Circle of Life

The words of

Grandfather James Dubray

Meta-Intelligence Institute
Franklin, North Carolina

I

Circle of Life
The Words of Grandfather James Dubray

Copyright © 2002 by Barbara Meister Vitale
Published by Meta-Intelligence Institute
Franklin NC.

Edited and Compiled by
Barbara Meister VItale

Cover Design by Richard Meister
Transcription/Editing by Patty Coleman
Setup and Production by Louis Vitale
ISBN: 979-889372128-7

II

To
Tunkasila

III

IV

Pilamayaye

I am honoring the wishes of Grandfather James Dubray that his words be preserved for his grandchildren and for future generations.
May his memory be honored by this book.

Much appreciation to the following:

Grandmother Florine Dubray for her loving support in being there from the taping, through the writing, and for sharing her stories.

Grandfather's children and grandchildren, for sharing their father and grandfather.

The Lakota people for keeping the Sacred ways.

Joe Brown Eyes for the Lakota language

Patty Coleman for transcribing, editing.

Richard Meister for the cover design/graphics.

Louis Vitale for hours of set-up and production.

Those who honored Grandfather by remembering their stories.

VI

Introduction

Although James Dubray called himself a common man, to many of us of all colors and races he was friend, father, teacher, uncle, Spiritual leader, and most of all Grandpa.

The following words give you a glimpse of who he was and is. Because he asked me not to change his words and to keep the Lakota syntax, sometimes the words may seem confusing, less than grammatically perfect, or have double meaning.

He said, "If they don't get it, then they aren't suppose to."

Grandpa often taught in circles or riddles. In his own words, "Now this is the hard part. You start listening over there, bout time you get there he's back over here. He starts up again and then he jumps ahead about his life and then he comes back. I don't know, it's going to take years before somebody really gets it straight. This'll come though."

Listen with your heart not your mind.

VIII

*Become a beautiful rainbow
and everything good will
be standing under you .*

Grandfather James Dubray

June 16, 1925
November 10,1999

IX

X

Thoughts of a Common Man

There have been many changes in my life. In 1974, I believe, or '75 Old Man Fools Crow, he said, "You take over. I'm going after Grandma and I'll be back and I'll take over tomorrow," he said. And tomorrow came and he came over and he said, "Give one of the boys a cigarette or something. Tell them to help you. Our drum is not ready so we'll be back." So they went along and probably about 4 years later came back to Kyle.

So this is what the old man, a teacher of mine, he taught me and he said, that you are the only man that we can find (We, not I, he said, but we) that you get along with all people, you never reject anyone and you're the *Waci itacan*, lead dancer. He said, "You're the head man dancer. Never wait for dark if anybody wants help at all hours, you help, you pray." "All you do is you pray," he said. "If you have your *Cannunpa*, your Peace Pipe ready, put tobacco in it, pray. If they have one, pray with them."

Later, they ask the chief how did this appear? Then he sang that song, *Tokaheya Wakan Tanka cewaki lo*; I pray to God that my people will live. He sang that song and after he sang, when he needs his help, he says, "*Kola le miye ca wau welo*; my friend, this is me that's coming." He never said, Grandfather or Father. He said, "my friend." So the word friend, *Kola,* means a lot.

Like my Circle started 1945, whatever, and after I'm gone the body stops but the Spirit keeps going. Because if there is a Spirit world, we're here now.

Just when I was born my Circle started. My Dad got his started, Mother combined the two, they gave me a Circle to start with. I'm supposed to take care of that. That's the only Circle I'll ever have, Circle of Life.

Dad was with me 21 years and he left and mother came along, of all my relatives, she is the only one that really knows me, 24 hours a day, my weak spots. She knows whether I'm strong or weak or better. My mother used to like to sing gospel songs, evening, it was peaceful, wood stove, kerosene lamp, very small cabin.

No one really knows my life. Grandma knows some things about me that no other people on planet earth know. Like I said my weak spots, my strong spots, how I secure my Circle. I have little circles out there.

I was probably 12 years old, 10 years old, I guess. The first time I seen Florine was when they brought her to school. I don't know how old she was. She had long braid. In front of Miss Caldwell I grabbed her by the hair and I pull her down. "Oh, teacher," I says to that teacher, "someday she's gonna be my wife." Oh boy, she grabbed my ear. In those days they used those yardsticks. They were kinda thick, ya know?

I got trapped into marrying Grandma. At that time Grandma was, ah, sweet 16 I believe. Yummy, yummy, yummy. Long hair, eyes are black like cherries and so forth. I don't see that no more. Anyway Uncle married us. You should have seen the vehicle I drove back, it was a 19, what is that, 28 Chevy. Two flat tires while driving, both left, one back and one front. Okay, that's the way her life started with me. Might say I've made many mistakes, made plenty. Try to correct them. She wasn't a mistake!

I didn't start preaching right after I married Grandma, not right after; first, to my brothers and sisters. But just like I said, I am about to find, remember, all the days together out of my life. About 2 years I wasted, on the road, off the road, try to be true to myself. Try to get myself to like me and love me before I can like anybody or love anybody. I have to get to know me. Then I probably start going to church, I left, ah, the Episcopal and went from there to Church of God, next Native American Church, I go. As a young man I always tell jokes, whatever it takes, I don't think let's just put that humor in it. Native American church, they used to have me talk mornings and tell them wild crazy stories. In Christian church it was about the same way. I found a gift and finally I worked. I could probably go any place out there. When I was 40, start going towards Native American traditional ways. Tried to go slow, tried to make myself understand. When I was in my 50's I tried to learn about the Seven Sacred Rites.

In my 60's I really tried to put it to work, started fasting, easy way and hard way of Sundance. And to bring to the people what I can do. The harder the way you pray the easier for the Spirit to work through you. I not only work with the *Cannunpa*, and *Hanbleceya* and Sundance and Sweatlodge, there are other things I have to learn. Most of my children, the two oldest ones they were brought up in churches, the rest of them the only thing they know is the Lakota Way. And these last two years they start baptizing their children in the Episcopal and one of them in the Presbyterian and one in Catholic. The only thing they know is pray Lakota every day.

You have that right to pray. Like going through a priest or anybody like that, I don't know about that. Lakota way they call freedom of religion you might say, I guess. And now it's kinda different. I met so many people but I never say I knew them. Later in years instead of Creator, everybody is a creator. You can create anything you want or the neighbor can create but I always say the Almighty God, *Wakan Tanka*, He is awesome, ya' know? And then Christianity, they brought Jesus Christ into our lives but I call him *Pejuta Ehannamani*, The Man That Walks With His Medicine. I still use him, He still uses me. I believe in Him and I'm pretty sure He believes in me. He knows my mistakes and He forgives me because He is full of love. I must have the love for people. Reject no one. Like the old timers tell me to reject no one, refuse no one. And I know I will be used many times over but that's how it is.

By the way, this summer at Sundance, don't laugh at me, I want to use florescent color. Same colors, black, yellow, red and white, but in florescent.

Yup. This is going to be a good one. I remember one of the boys, two years ago, he had green on. He said this way I want *Tunkasila* to recognize me. Here he passed on. That Floyd wants to go in but he can't prance around like he used to, knee surgery. He did some crazy things but remember all the good things these people did, ya' know. People change.

Won't be like Bear Butte, Sundance time. We'll try to get a couple of those huge tanks, 1,000 gallons. Well, let's hope. Some are suppose to work on that. Have to practice that!

Tree of Life, so hopefully someone will bring some cottonwood trees even though three or four are planted down that creek. It don't take long. The cottonwood tree has a star in each branch? Like a star the shape of a heart. What's that other one they cut, Birch, Poplar or whatever? They're the same thing.

I always prayed Sundance, there'd just be twelve or ten. Maybe this year will be it. I'll try to bring the *Cannunpa* to one maybe it'll happen this year. Whatever, whatever, everything will be okay. The third day I guess we'll just go ahead and have our doctoring. I'll pick some young men to do that but, huh! They go in to know, become like God, to become God, but they know nothin, they come out like babies, but maybe they already are God.

Exorcism, it comes in. I've seen so many, many, many things. One year there was a young lady, there was something in her back, it moved and you could hear it from her mouth. "Stay away from me!" in that deep voice. Florine got scared and my brother, Bat, got scared and a few of the boys. I'd like somebody to stand by me when those things happen. Maybe they'll see something or hear something. It's pretty scary sometimes. Especially when they wash your feet with 7-Up. Remember that time, Sundance, she wash my feet, not water. Boy, was I surprised. Florine's fired. She's no nurse, no more.

I might pick one of the young men to take over so I can do more work. I'll be free to do other things besides trying to hold it together twelve months a year. Maybe I could get two young men in there and they can hold that Circle together. Maybe we do a little campaigning for *Tunkasila*. Keep them on God for as long as we can, cause, after all, He created all things but there are other people trying to move in His territory.

You know that there are two representatives, one is sitting on each of your shoulders. "Do this, this is right way" and the other one said, "No, don't do, he's wrong." If you're weak, you listen to the wrong one and you'll be doing something else.

When you hear that sound, noise like, you know, like a tone, listen. That's Gray Eagle sitting on your left trying to tell you something, try to understand, after a while, you'll understand it. He's going to teach you about things on the right side. You'll never know which side he'll stand. He'll tell you one way, the way of the old man. He said to tell them, "You're okay, you have tried. Listen, you've tried this and it didn't work, so now try this other way. Maybe it will work for you." That's where experience, they say is good teacher. But sometimes it hurts with experience. It's suppose to come through elders. Those suppose to advise, they've been through, the so-called has-beens. They've been there. Be careful that tone is two, one is sharp and one ain't so sharp. And it can approach you maybe three, four times a day maybe dozen times a day. Through an animal, a bird, or maybe some person. The ugliest that can come to you may be a drunken person and he may be it. The kindest one, the prettiest one, that approaches you, that's the time to be careful. It can turn itself into the most beautiful thing in the world, so when the Lakota says *Wakan* Sica, how ugly it is, but you turn that, it's the most beautiful thing. I saw people just go after that. It makes you feel good, pretend it's making you feel good, but afterwards you don't feel so good. You can see that with some of girls. Ahhh, they fell in love, the man they fell in love with, I looked at him, my goodness gracious. I must say, that's all I'm going to say. Same with the boys and yet I guess that's the best they can do.

What I'm always looking for is people that can carry out responsibility without looking over their shoulder. They can go for it, if they have someone that's there and there is trust between the two. That they don't have to give an account of every move he makes or she makes.

So to work for *Tunkasila* it's a very hard thing. But if you have one that's a non-believer, you have to give account every time someone comes along. They ask you, "what did he say, what did she say?" And those are confidential. This person otta know that this is it. It's very hard. And some people that are called to come in, have worked with the *Cannunpa*, and yet, they have problems. I have problems, but not like theirs. They talk about drug and alcohol and so forth. The family's in it too. Marriage break-up, or whatever. And you can't save them all. The only thing you can do is you tell them, and if they say, "I am a man," or "I am a woman," now then that's what they are. But to me they are just a bunch of little kids. Yet they have so much to learn, lot to learn, even the older ones. The boys, they come pretty close to finding the Great Spirit. And yet they are hanging onto something back there. Material things, maybe, of some sort.

You can talk about Mickey Mouse, make up a story that'll make sense to that young kid in their later years, there's a story in it that's a parable of some sort. You take all those cartoons, there is a lot of violence in it. Popeye the sailor man, Mutt and Jeff, and what's his name, that jackrabbit or the bunny and the coyote and the beep-beep runner and whatever, roadrunner. And that's all of us. So we see a cartoon and those kids sitting there laughing, but we ourselves we're seeing ourselves and these little kids are laughing at us, like Popeye the sailor man and Olive, she's so ugly and skinny and all that. And that what's-his-name, Buford? Brutus? Bruno? Or something like that. You know some of us we feel like that. Huge! Fighting over Olive, just to upset Popeye the sailor man. But to me there are lessons in all of them. There are some Lakota stories just like that, *Inkto, Iktomi* stories. Those are right there. Lakota's are just a common people, wandering around the plains, woodlands; always move close to water and trees.

Pte San Wi . Pte San Wi means not white, it means gray, like Grandma's hair,

There are different people you've met, all kinds, you know they all don't belong to one church, but to me church, those are organizations. They are organized and before long they gave themselves a name, another starts and there are little tiny circles all around like the Almighty talked about. Just imagine how huge that big one is and all those little ones going around. No wonder we are so sickly. We inhale germs out there, we inhale death and other things, good and bad, we inhale. These are the things that the almighty God does, stopped hurting many, many years ago. And He gave us fresh, the air is fresh right now, look at all that snow out there. And the sky is not blue it's gray, but just between those two colors we talk about the Buffalo Woman.

In Lakota they call it *Pte San Wi* . *Pte San Wi* means not white, it means gray, like Grandma's hair, gray, there. It's gray.

There is a Buffalo up there, gray. But that old lady came down and said, "I'm the Buffalo Woman, White Buffalo Woman, I have brought you life," last summer. How can she bring me life when I already have life? My life, my Circle started in 1925. I don't know how old she is but there is a good lesson there too, out of this. And bless her heart for bringing, coming in late of year and saying, "I brought you good, brought you life." Now this, what she said, I brought you life, this woman I don't know. I never shook hands with her, she never sleep with me so how could she bring me life? Now these are facts of life we are talking about. So how can she give me life when already I had a woman that she give me some lives, four boys and four girls? You understand what I am saying? So this woman, I don't know, she says, "I brought you life." I don't think she can take care of me, wash my clothes, cook for me. It takes three or four women to do that. One keep house, one cook, one wash dishes, one tend to my grand kids. In fact, it probably take dozen women to do that. How can one person bring life and yet, She can.

She didn't notice me. I mean she didn't know who I am. She comes to Lakota Nation and she don't know because there's lots of pretenders, imitators, and as the white man, call Shaman. I am not one of those. I'm not an imitator. To me this is real, it's the real thing. And each one is going to have to give an account. When the Great *Tunkasila* said, there was this woman with this crown, you go the other way. So every day appreciate, I don't care what kind of weather we get, it's good. And if you say today is bad weather. You missed a good weather day. See if you can give us one better than Almighty God. So these things we have to go along with.

Gray Eagle sits on left shoulder and right shoulder; he approaches you in many ways. So take your mind off of things. I'll be going down the road and I do a lot of thinking and everyone will be talking. I turn around, the radio is soft music or Peyote music or Pow Wow, and I just drive. Whatever it is that talks to me, talks to my brains and my heart, many things come through me. It's like, I don't know how it does it, especially in a car. That's like sitting in some jail cell going down the road and that holy thing, little tiny box, keeping that engine going. But yesterday, how many cars can they make that turn in and out of that place and you women still don't understand. How can this little, all of a sudden this car got so tiny that she made these turns, while those cars are spinning, this car didn't spin. Maybe this car is *Wakan*, I don't know. But whoever made it they pray about this, these things, before it started. I didn't want to go all the way out there. I still don't understand why. But when I go I want people to make it easier for themselves. Don't take me clear out into the boon docks. Pray hard that it won't be like summer time, July or August or lightening and thunder, or winter time blizzard. There is four seasons.

I hope to be around at least another 30 years to give everybody hell every chance I get. So we create that hell. We'll get there, wherever, to that heaven or happy hunting grounds. That's only second stage in life, you know. That's the last one, after that, the real one, we'll get to see the colored marbles and yet I've seen the marbles already, in that cave. So what kind of marble are we going to see that's been written about in the Holy Bible? We reading that Bible two chapters a day. In one year you can go through the whole thing. Verse by verse, it's going to take you a lot of time. You read it many, many times over and still won't know nothing.

So when that so-called *Pejuta Gluhamani* man was walking with His medicine, He came to the Lakota people, the savages, that's when we taught Him how to pray. He didn't have no book. His life was the book of life. The Circle of Life, the bread of life, the *mni-wi-co-ni,* water of life. We had it all. And people didn't understand. Up to this day, many times He comes to us. Every day He is here with us and we don't see Him.

Sometimes we sit and we gossip. I'm guilty of that now and then, but I always go around. It's easy to forgive, but never forget so that it will never happen again. All these other people that talked, they misused me. It's my fault and I pray that it will all be there. Put away the differences. There are some people way younger than I am that try to use race as prejudice while I'm trying to do God's work in a certain way. Not Episcopal, Catholic or traditional, *Cannunpa,* whatever. God has made all these things for us to use to bring us closer to Him and He even promised that He'd die for us. Each one of us must do that, die for Florine or the kids, I must do that. Do not take drugs. Do not take all this and that. The rules of Christianity are so many. The *Cannunpa* way is simply you organize, have discipline, respect and humble yourself.

It's called Peace Pipe, *Cannunpa.* It's a Spiritual. In each hand as we go along, as we go along sposed to become *Wakan.* That's what that song said. Everyday and years ago, I don't know too much, I'm only 72 years, Circle I talk about is twenty, thirty, forty, fifty, sixty, seventy, eighty, ninety, and three more years of that, and I'm still seventy-two. This is what it's all about. It gives us life, it gives us health.

I died twice, 1957. I knew it all. I was a minister, first time I was at Salvation Army. I couldn't afford it. Someone gave Salvation Army a pair of pants. They charged me about three or four dollars and a shirt, oh, I liked this white shirt, all colors a black tie and I had a Bible, um um. Pastor said, " James, brother James, will you bring the message?" I got up like this. Oh, I know all the chapters and verses, everything there but God so loved the world, that He gave His only begotten son, who-so-ever ... then I stopped. I didn't know. A year later both my lungs collapsed. I had two hundred people working on me, fifty-five thousand dollars borrowed, one year it was forty-five thousand, eight times is that much. Ninety six days later I came out, out of there.

I had nothing but I was taught how to pray. A little tiny ant, some of you know, some of you maybe not, ant hill or poison. Those little creatures are all over the US. It's eyes huge and there was my little soul ready to go, no tomorrow. That was when I went back to school, twenty years old. But when I got out of there it took me thirty-six months, 4 years older I guess. The embarrassing thing is when I first went back at my age there was an 18 yr. old boy. He was tutoring me. Two weeks later I had 14 people, a black man he like to tell jokes. The white man he didn't like paper work, the Mexican moved just swiftly but for many hours. Their influence was out there. But the Indian he did his trick and got out of there in 36 months. No fancy outfit, no Eagle feathers, no star quilt, no nothing back home to be straightened out. I didn't have time to stand there and have some principal or superintendent kiss you on the cheek, that day will come.

I came back one year there were non-denominational churches. Oh, that was good. I do everything I can, I didn't even know they were there until a few days I heard blah, blah, blah and on and on. Till one day there's an elderly whose sick, a nephew come. I'm going after Grandpa. I didn't know nothing. He said, "You watch and tomorrow he's goin after the Holy Tree. Come up." But I should have said no. I should have made excuses. Ohhhh.

Young people always look for power. Wanna be the top man. And by the way, I never found a boss, a top man, whatever, only Almighty God. It seems like everywhere I go I end up supervising, coordinating. I'm the one that's always catchin' heat, I should have said catchin' hell. Later I thought I was. He was pretty smart. I thought if he can I can, then lose my mind. Went home and he never did come back. What happened to Uncle Fools Crow? Andrew Fools Crow his name, Frank Fools Crow. He took care of us. What happened to Mack Elk? These elders sit and get along with all people. Never reject anyone. They have love for you, some of you probably know, have love for me take you with me over half century. From that to where I'm at and I used to study the Bible, two chapters a day, one year of that by time I finish I still don't know nothing. I didn't receive something. Oh, from there I went chapter, verse and goin this way. Somehow he said that almost passed it. Maybe I'll become a Holy Man, *Tunkasila Wakan.*

One of my uncles he save us, there was medicine there. He was up there. Oh shoot, you know they already laid that rope and I didn't know, pray for me. Before you know one day I stood there in Los Angeles with a Holy Bible chapter 8 Romans and this woman have cancer. He said he was going to send her home and I could visit every weekend. Well, I stood there cause I didn't know. Someone came in with a pretty blue coat, ya know, white and stood along side of him, cause I didn't know I thought at that time a lady. I wouldn't have known anything but elders were there they said, "hallelujah, praise the lord," and all and so forth. They must have felt that air again, some power, I didn't.

Everything that's Lakota on this island is all recorded in that Bible. There is one I like, is Ezekiel that old name. He tell us about the Lakota. Here, I lost my story, he says look at that one facing the East praying for the sun commin up. He turned, faces West praying for the tree, He looked down at His rocks, and He prayed for the rocks. He prayed to the water. He said my son, I created all things. He prayed to All My Relations. He said, I have a name. You seen this wagon wheel, so forth, this Circle. The spokes, each one a man made rule, of this church, like a medicine wheel and He said they forgot. That Circle never give in, but never come together because only I will. Someone has to go out and tell before it's too late and you think billions and billions of people how we gonna fit in there in His heart.

They say every organization, churches organized, and started calling it culture, cults. But it's Lakota traditional, you all have traditional. Your great grandparents, their traditional, the way they pray, out of respect. On my Dad's side his grandpa had five wives and on mothers side the name of the elders American Boy, America Horse, he had four wives and here I only have a friend, barely even see her.

Have you testified for God, have you had anything good happen that He did? All the glory goes to Him. I didn't do anything. It came through Him, to Him, through me. *Tunkasila* worked always to see it that way. I guess, all I have to ask Him, is to touch people. Some want to do crazy movement or paint or whatever and have visions, but I've got those things. You've got to be careful. Make sure it's the Holy Spirit that does the work, ya know! They call it the Holy Ghost I guess.

I need some time too, to be myself. I don't want to do anything, but I sure want to eat pretty soon. Now this is the hard part. You start listening over there, bout time you get there he says he's back over here. He starts up again and then he jumps ahead about his life and then he comes back. I don't know, it's going to take years before somebody really gets it straight. This'll come though.

So much happened that His, my family is fine. When I say my family your looking at, at least 100 nations. Your looking at 17,000 or 18,000 Sundancers that comes through. Somehow some are still here and that one is still here. They want to catch more hell, I guess.

So when you get to other side there will be no hell, because hell is here already. Then He'll make paradise here, but we're not talking about hell or paradise we're talking about Spirit World and we're all going to be there in the Spirit World. When we all get there I don't know how long we'll wait for the Master to come, the Creator Himself. And that's the death.

When someone takes that road, walks over to that beautiful place we honor that one. Dress them beautiful, send personal medicine things with them, that's theirs. The relatives give everything away to his friends that way. They will see that and remember him. Everyone gets fed, lots of birthday cakes, this is that one's birth, not other way. Some give star quilts, blankets, other stuff to honor. Real honor is remembering, living what was taught, walking your talk.

Right now this death means freedom but there will be more. I don't have much teeth and Grandma don't have many, but when we go there, there will be those gnashing or bashing their teeth and crying and wishing they were dead. When I think about the short time you people know little about me, nobody really don't know me. Nobody really don't know me. Florine only know me about 50 years, she really don't know me, my kids don't know me.

In 1957 a sister, Catholic nun, walked me to door and she pointed, that's your wife and those are your children. They brought Tommy in as a babe and I didn't know him but I said, "okay." They call that reborn, I guess, I was dead but then again I was given a chance. I just recognized my grandmother. She was in there. They accused her of giving me peyote or some kind of drug, that's why I kept getting sick. And she accused the doctors of giving me too much drugs, so I didn't recognize people.

Well, maybe God went and changed me, ya know. They call that reborn again. After my heart surgery, I understand they came to me took me to that place. I didn't realize there were so many people out there, 8 years ago or 9 years ago at Bear Butte. Floyd

I am a Human Being just like anybody else.

Hand came up and he told people stay away, don't touch him. I was walking down towards the Sweatlodge. One of the Grandmas, she said, "No one is going to him. That's my baby brother." She came and she hugged me, they couldn't stop her. Her husband was standing, he couldn't come, nobody could. There was a big crowd at that time. I was walking through the aisle of people standing on both sides all the way. I'm so important ya know. Like if I am important or I'm a savior or some sort of a prince or whatever. I didn't recognize no one and yet I went from here to there. I had to start recognizing people and get to know people all over again. And right now, like today that crowd, there's few I remember. It's my life. It's different from ten years ago even last year. I am a Human Being just like anybody else, I have feelings. I hurt. Sometimes I feel good and sometimes I want to be alone. Today I can think clearly.

An incident happened here last year I believe. I walked, Steve's little one was with me. I walked in the kitchen, I got me a cup of coffee and I was gonna get milk out of the fridge. I went to grab at that handle, my hand just went all the way through it. Wait a minute. I start staggering. I looked at the coffee; there was no coffee in it. The cup was empty, so what happened to that coffee? I started talking to little Stevey and he didn't understand. It's a language, but it's not English, it's not Lakota. Maybe God? The first language that came out was only one language. I was told that many languages came after that.

I tried my best to open the fridge again and here my hand it went on through. My hand was just like so. I looked and here my hand, my arm was hanging and another arm was there also. This was the one I kept using and there's nothing there. It was just like the shirt

I had on, the same thing. So for a while there I had three arms, two on my right and one my left. And I grabbed the phone and that phone went on through. I dropped the phone so I had to use my left hand. There was a package of cigarette on the coffee table, I grabbed it and the cigarette went on through, the cigarette lighter went on through my hand. About that time Grandma must have took off. We couldn't call, Little Stevey didn't know how to call. Tom came a running but when I talked to him he didn't understand.

Before you know there's lots of people in there. Some of my cousins were there that had been in Christian Church and heard that unknown tongue, a long tongue, or no tongue they call it. In church, you know the Holy Ghost comes, Holy Spirit comes and they use people. Someone said, "No, that isn't it. Something happened here." So they smudged.

They called Steve. He was working at Batesland. So instead, coming back he went off to Martin then he came back and Grandma came back with Squeaky. So I told her, "Get my *Cannunpa*. The Elk Pipe." And I had a hard time, trying to make her understand what I wanted, I tried, take that Elk *Cannunpa* and put tobacco in it and bring me the *Cannunpa* so I can pray or smoke. No this running here and there. Finally, I had to motion, ya know, and she brought it. Steve came back and in just about an hour Bat pulled in. They had an *Inipi,* Sweatlodge for me. I told Florine, I said, "I might have to leave you but take care of yourself and of those who can't take care of themselves because something's happened to me. My Spirit wants to go, it's time.

We're in the Sweatlodge and they prayed for me, different people come ya know. Then Bat came in the evening and had a Sweatlodge. He said, I was gone but God had some things for me to do so He put my Spirit back into my body. God said, I would be all right but I had to do these things I was given to do. He has a lot of work to do.

Some how, with that strength, I was getting stronger. I would never ever forget that. I had seen my Spirit partially came out of my body. If I had laid there and I'd been standing there they would never have seen me, but they would have seen my body, the body that I used to live with. Things are gonna change and I talk about it. Nobody listens. I used to be right handed but now I'm left handed, a south paw. So we'll see, time will tell.

 **Man was made before the *Cannunpa* and the *Cannunpa* was made before time.**

I was talking bout how the *Cannunpa* exits. Okay, *Wakan Tanka, Tunkasila,* He created all things first, even the animal, everything. Then He said, it was good, *waste.* But without Him there is nothing there, so what

24

did He Create first? Man was made before the *Cannunpa* and the *Cannunpa* was made before time. Man was with God and God was with man and He said, "Let us make man in our image." And He said nothin' bout a woman. He said, let us make man, *Wicasa unkagapi kte*, so we must be like puppets, ya' know or what? Good puppets, robots.

He said, "Let us, *Hiyupo tokeya Wicasa tokeca wanji iyececa unkaga*, let us make a man like ourselves." So, is there more than one God? His family, He said let us, *Hiyupo*, come on. So He must have a whole bunch of people working with him and all this, He said is, "good." Then Adam comes in the picture again. In all this universe He put us here, and He looked at it and said, "it's good." Now where did this God come from? Where did *Tunkasila* come from? How small we are, but how huge is out here. Is it crumbled all there within our body? Look at those little midgets, those little kids, babies, *Wakanyeja*, the Holy Child. That's tomorrow, that little baby I just talked about. These are Holy and when they're around we got to watch this tongue, what we say or how we act.

So He try to teach us the good things and He give us advice. There is a season, a time for everything. The animals have time for a mate, mating and we must like-wise. We are supposed to have dominion over it all. Physical, Spiritual we can make them do whatever we want. When we go near an animal or bird it takes off.

What have we become? Because we took the wrong turn. So we become violent, just like that movie with that iron rifle, whatever it is.

Then Adam comes in the picture again. Now wait a minute, he's weak, so God created a woman. It said, we'll take part of him and they be one. So they become one, but something went wrong. This woman had seen the mating of the animals and she think it's time for them to practice that and see how it feels. She said, *Lecanuki Wakan Tanka* ... you going to become like dog and you going to create the problems yourselves, you going to become a god. You be creating the problems, you choose yourself, like anything else they talk and talk and before they know it those two got together and they mate and a baby was born. They didn't wait very long and another one was born and that's where good and bad they come from. These two had an argument, brother and sister, even now days, over little things.

Two sisters can argue. Now days it's money. They argue over money. *Tunkasila* already set this down there to see if these two really love each other or love this so called *Tunkasila* they create. All of a sudden these two will argue or these two men will argue, like nothing happen again they come together. And that was how it happened, way back there.

This Turtle Island, we've been here for all time, thousands of years. Scientists say, fossils show this turtle was under water. Later, the Lakota people said they were already here, then great flood come.

My Grandmother said these things. A chief was there when the water came up, the flood in the Bible. It happened fast, but he knew to take, grab, a young beautiful woman, and they found this tree. The water came, cleaned everything. The chief he knew how to survive, so he became an Eagle, *wambli,* and took that beautiful woman to top of hill. When water went back to where it came, they flew down. That Eagle picked a woman for his mate and came back. She became a woman and he became a man and creation started again. They came together and made children and grandchildren, and great-grandchildren. These, the chief and beautiful woman, are the ancestors. All bad animals, dinosaur, whatever, all drowned. Now scientists say we come around to this island, but we say, no, we were already here, 10, 15, 20,000 years.

The *Cannunpa* came because they forgot.

The master, *Wanikiya* this living thing, He said, this generation will not pass. They told Lakota talked about this, *Pejuta Gluhanani,* He will teach you all things, the man who walks with His medicine will teach you all things. He will know the seven sins and the seven sacred things. The *Cannunpa* came because they forgot.

The Lakota forgot what He told them to do. Go on top of hill and pray like I ask. I'm here and I'm with you always. You have it. So this woman came to remind them. So every Holy thing comes through a woman. Everything comes from a woman, the *Cannunpa,* Jesus, children. That star, She has power to bring life. That respect you remember without her you would not be. Even the Creator, Grandfather, I think, has one, come from a woman, maybe someday I'll know, see Her up there when I leave.

The woman has to be a virgin and she picks a man. That man stands along side of her until it's over and then they become one. Now this is a mystery. No offense to nobody. Long time ago, Lakota man and woman, they become one and if they separate, they split the woman's nose with a knife. Wherever she goes, she's a failure at that home. She takes off, *Ho-o-ka-winh waku we.* You know what a hobo is? Go here and there. Go man to man. And finally comes back to that home and he takes her in, back in. I'm looking for a big family. She's left that family. She went all around and she comes back to that family. These should have been told last 30, 40 or 50 years but since a new system started nobody did. They call it common law wife. Anymore you can live with someone 30 days, 2 weeks go to another man or another woman. *Witkowin,* that's a crazy woman. In plain English, become a whore they call it, sleep with anybody. Man likewise. None of that will enter the Spirit world. They will not answer the Spirit world. These things should have been told.

This is where I need teachers to talk to the young girls before they start to try and throw the ball. Not four days, maybe four years maybe forty years then that lady can throw the ball. *Tapa kahol iyaye,* or *Tapa yeyapi,* they call it. Throwing the ball. So it's just not about a girl thinking about her monthly that's coming like constant everyday. Now that teacher gets drunk or runs around, gossips, whatever, that same girl she's holding ceremony for, she's influencing. Making of the boy, same way. Making of a man.

I love my kids. Not with just words but with all my heart. Not bottom of my heart, bottom is very little bit. I love you from the bottom of my heart. That's about empty now, scraping the barrel, looking for love, what little they find they say they love me with that. No one ever come and say with all my heart.

Many times I ask myself if I happen to go this year or next two or three years all these people say they love me and all that right now, hanging on to that tree, after I'm gone will they keep loving my wife, my children, my grandchildren or will they just leave it.

Then later, that cross came into the picture. Then the *Cannunpa* came in. Somebody has to pay for it. So when you grab that cross somebody is there with loving open arms. He'll die for you, He'll take all the sick, carry on His shoulders so you can go on ahead. In life, never do it again. You do it you may die there. That's the way with the *Cannunpa*. She said, "Do not play. *Ma-gna-ye-sni yo*, don't fool me. This is *Wakan* and I gave it to this Lakota man." Cause he is wandering the plains. He didn't have no land, nothing. So She give him this. So the Christians really don't own nothing. Truly a Christian, they can't say this is my house, this is mine, this is *le mi ta wa*, my land. Cause they are lying if they do. Everything belongs to Him. So some of the crazy people go and share their love and never think about tomorrow, tomorrow will take care of itself.

But everything goes with a song. You have a pretty voice. You don't think so but you have. You all have pretty voices, in your way. Never think highly of yourself. Stay in the background and somebody will say, "hey?" The first will come last and the last will come first. And now the *Cannunpa* is everywhere. One language is everywhere.

30

All my relations, *Mitaku Oyasin*, do they know what they are saying? You talk about that little tiny ant, that cockroach that you kill, that's part of your relation. God created that. It's like with flyswatter, we start killing. Because, we're angry people, we are ready to kill anything. Maybe they are poor. They can't afford so you help. I've been to many homes. They have laws, man-made rules, man-made laws and they become a God cause they got you in their nest. They want you to do the things and say the things they want you to do and say, but the Lakota he say, "*Tima hiyu na catku ta iyotaka yo,* come on in." Go to the back room and from that back room you work your way around. That's the best she or he has. They don't have guest room. The man who give up his room, the woman who give up her bed, that's her best. That's the Lakota way. That's our life, the way we live.

Like Chancey, with blond hair and all that but he speaks Lakota. There is more power in that *Takoja* than a lot of those big medicine man out there or wanna-be's. Indians they wanna-be. Everybody wants to be a wanna-be. Instead of these and that we are gonna be a wanna-be nation one of these days. Everybody wants to be a wanna-be something.

When I'm an old man, maybe I'll become a medicine man, or maybe I'll be a spiritual leader. I've been dead how many times, 3 or 4 times already, 3 times anyway. I seen the Spirit from beyond come and I saw his hand. I saw myself with three arms. Maybe someday I'll be a spiritual leader. But I can never be a holy man because all mighty God will come and *Tunkasila*, He is the only *Wakan*. At Sundance time I sure can knock'em down. Always make sure that you are capable and strong enough to go in and dance with the sun if not stay behind, learn.

You never reject anyone.

I'm lucky. I have my four girls and four boys, grand kids around except my oldest. He's in Spirit world, he comes and goes. There's another granddaughter over there nobody really knows, was 5, 6, 7 months old when she came early. That's why I always choose a boy and a girl at the beginning of time. Somebody, two people are saviors out of my life. One is Christianity and one is Lakota, Lakota Way. They both end up with God. We gotta be careful what we say about people because He felt bad about it. He did some good things in life. He just can't shut the door on those people. Others did some good things. He helped. They all helped. And one little mistake and everyone blah, blah, blah. What about themselves? You gotta pick-up every chip around your house before you come down on someone. That's not my way. When you have that love for people that means you either gossip or no gossip. Don't put it into words like that. You can point finger and that finger comes back to you. That's all that matters.

Some say, get to see everybody at that beautiful shore. That's Spirit world. And they said in Christianity, that He walked on water. So how many is gonna walk with Him when He comes to that shore and cross on over? Lakota when *Mni-wi-co-ni* comes in there be water. Winter time I walk on water, ice. Really look at, it's water, ice. Anybody's gonna say I love you, now is the time to say if they love me hang onto my words. Trying to share my Circle of life, love people. Doesn't matter who he is, what kind of person. Maybe the reason why I was picked for this position is that like that old man says, we chose you, we picked you because you get along with people. You never reject anyone. And I didn't know anything about this Circle. I was like some of boys. I guess I held back for a long time, finally, I got in and I'm not ashamed of it.

My words, my life, it's all open. Sometimes my own family, immediate, they don't understand. But it's like Florine and I were together. Surely one day our kids they'll be together; think as one. It starts at home. And if they don't listen just continue on, somebody else will listen. One moves out a dozen or more will come in.

This year I have met so many people, too many. And this coming summer ceremony who knows how many will be there. And I know I will be criticized. But so far, God and *Tunkasila* is with me. I don't care who is against me. What they think. Cause when the white man came we accept all this, electricity, fence, building, school. But *Tunkasila* said take the good, leave the bad. But too many of them picked up the bad. Now it's time to go back and pick up the good things of life that we can go into the future with it. Traditionally, they call it traditional; this is our traditional time, my time, my children's time, my grandchildren's traditional time. In history, whatever has been back there take it and now. Take what is good here and go into the future to help someone. Next 30, 40 or 50 years all this is going to change. The future there might be a mini-mart here in Kyle to begin with. Might be a hospital here. In Allen, we might have few other businesses; like a skyscraper here. Who knows?

Every time somebody does something wrong to me or the family I always say thank you because something is there, I learn something from it. The negative things I take and sometimes it's a good thing, turn out to be good. I had open heart surgery, there's couple of women went with me that year or maybe more and each year winter time they go instead of me. I go and check up on them and they come and visit me. Always want to know how I'm doing, what I'm doing and all that, that goes with it. Those people are gone and I'm still here.

That song that was sung here, that's a beautiful song, traditional Lakota song. Each one of us has a song that God gave it to *Tunkasila*. There is a *Wasicu,* white woman, as they call themselves, even though she is not white she stood there. She is pinkish color, but they call it white. She *Hanbleceya,* fasted. What? On second or third day somebody taught her a song and she sang it and she wasn't ashamed. Only thing she sang it in English, she is very humble. I talked to her and asked her or told her that before she did this I had said, "Someone here I'm going to pick a lady to sing a song, sing me a song for all of us. You all be ready," I said. And just like saying it is. Even the old lady she thought I was going to ask her to sing. So she probably was preparing herself. And I know in her mind what song she was going to sing. But I asked this lady, I pointed at her and I said you sing this song. "Who me? I never sing."

I said, "Yeah, you." And she got up and she start singing a song. One verse and she said, "I don't know." I said, "Try again. Maybe it'll come this time." She looked around, she said, "I need help. Will some of you stand and help me sing." Few, at first, then they all got up, everybody. And she started singing. How does that song go? It's Beautiful America. And that little grandson, from the back he sort of moved up front when I talked about border to border, coast to coast, and turtle island, south and north. Now we have other people coming from all over the world to this beautiful place, so called America. And that's the song she sang. And I don't know this woman but I sure got a big hug for it, and she kissed my ear. So I made a joke. I don't mind if a man hug me but the women that hug they start kissing my ear, now they're coming too close to my lip.

I went to that cave. It was recorded the last time it was occupied, I mean without electricity and all that about ten thousand years ago. And I think one of the boys said, the Lakota people were here twenty thousand years ago or better. And this is where the so called *Wanikiya*, the Christ, the Savior, the Messiah, Jesus Christ had come to teach all. And, in that book, that's how He came with the Calf Pipe and She showed Him how, taught Him to pray like He did.

So this is why it is always taking them back to that granddaughter and grandson. And sometimes in that Sweatlodge that beautiful voice sings. Maybe I'm the only one that hears Her sing. And that young man He comes to visit me. Long hair, sometimes it's in braids, He wraps himself with red shawl, whatever, around His waist or shoulder, beautiful soft buckskin leggings. He has a hand drum and He sings and He follows me, He went with me to North Carolina. He sat next to me, smiling and I forget whether it was green or blue bandanna. He had it on like a sweatband. And I think I told there, that a Lakota is here. I don't know if it's a Cherokee or what. I put it that a way.

So somebody is always with me. And this is kinda part of my life. Maybe I was many, or many are called or maybe I was one that was chosen. But I respect all the men and women that say they are medicine man or medicine woman. Hope they can put it into words for me with the power they have. The important thing is that if we are the medicine man and the spiritual leader, holy man, that sickness and problems that come, if we pray hard, maybe it won't happen, maybe we'll all learn something from it. Hold days for our prayers. Believe in our prayers. And I think of all those that spent a few days with me, and so far they forgot to feed me breakfast this morning. I'm gettin' hungry. That's going to help our people? My voice needs a rest, let my better half talk a while.

When one, one of my son's was really sick, I was going here and there with him. I prayed and I said, "Please don't take my son away." I said, "Make him be a man. He's going to be a good man some day. If you want I'll take his place." And I said, "But wait till my baby son gets about 15 or 16 years old, then you could take me." and I said that. Then I thought why did I say that? Maybe my son will live anyway. I went on and on.

I was at the hospital with him when his Dad went over there and got him out of there. We'd go from place to place, and every time I'd go along. So I went, they had a Sundance. They took him down there to that Sundance. The poor thing, he didn't even have no hair. He was skin and bones. He ran down the creek, I looked and here he went down a creek and got water and came back to the Sweatlodge. Pretty soon there was whole bunch of people coming in there, he was in that bunch. They made him sit one place and that and here. I stood there and prayed and I never prayed so hard in my life cause I never lost nobody.

All a sudden I seen a white cloud coming down, coming right down. That was my first vision. It came down and here I looked again. I stood there watching and here it was a white Buffalo. It came down, not on the ground, just straight down. The Spirits picked up my son, he was dancing, and they just put him on the back of that Buffalo. He was going round and round and round right up toward the skies and then my son was coming back. They were bringing him back. I think it was about the third round when he was coming back.

I was sittin' there thinking, oh, this is it, ya know, I thought to myself. Hey, he came back. He's coming back and here I looked and he had a long pretty war bonnet on. He was smiling and waving at everybody. I cried, "Oh, he's coming back," I said, "He's going to make it." Boy, he was really happy. He danced and I didn't see nothing, I just sat there and prayed. I looked and here, he was really dancing. He had strength. Poor thing, he was just skin and bone and here he was just really dancing hard. His brother was dancing beside him. There was a lot of people but his brother was there right beside him. Everything he did his brother had to do because he was right there beside him. It was real scary!

They should have a picture of me. We have no picture of ourselves, not even when I was a young kid. Then the log house where Lulu and Florine and I was and then the one house we used to live where Isabel was, we used to live there. And we moved to the other one. So my life is like a gypsy. I don't know what a gypsy is but I think of a gypsy. So when you work for *Tunkasila*, when He picks you, you become that. When it's time to move it's time to move.

When this is all set up, the arbor and the whole thing I wish that all I pray for are all those people that have used me. I hope they are all there and still be in the physical they can come in this time and see *Tunkasila*'s power, how much power He has when you are chosen or when you're picked or chosen whichever way. Cause many are called and maybe they were called to do one item but they exaggerated without stopping, without knowing, or without realizing they went on, lost it all. Lost it all.

Sort of this is just me talking. I think yesterday Spirit was talking. I thought I had sore throat or whatever, ya know? And so far I haven't coughed yet, did I? Maybe that come again. I don't know. Or maybe I'm still at home and this is somebody else driving you people towards Rapid. Maybe you are still sleeping, dreaming. Who knows? It's a good day, beautiful day. But you don't ever see that like that again. Tomorrows gonna change. In a few hours, that will change. Everything's gonna change.

With me hanging around, Florine has suffered many, many years. At the beginning and third year of our lives, she started out with polio and that went away. Later years they said cancer and that went away. Physically, five or six years ago I believe, and you know Spiritually. I think I'll have a cigarette since I haven't coughed any. It be just like that one young man

So when you work for *Tunkasila*, when He picks you, you become that.

that showed up. Came asking about skeleton and up to this day he could see people like those Lakota men standing in there that just went there for one purpose, to buy alcohol. That is a no, no because they don't know Christianity, they heard about the Lakota way but they never tried, they never were taught. I never said, I will reappear.

She herself, White Buffalo Woman said, "I will be back one day." Some say come back as a baby or as an old cow, Buffalo, pig. She must be an elderly woman that brought the *Cannunpa* but She appeared to them as a young, beautiful lady. When She left She rolled over and the gray one standing there. And that's where the colors come in. People add on to it. Yellow, black, red and white and then the blue sky, the green grass, the browns. Brown represents the Spirits. And all those people didn't care for brown but maybe the Holy Spirit become Godly, then they start wearing different colors. Nobody cares for brown I think. Maybe some people like brown. And there is the orange, the yellow. All shades of different colors, *Wigmuke*, the rainbows are there. Milky Way, the *Wanagi Tacanku* they call it, the Spirit trail. When someone dies the Spirit goes to the Spirit world. They say, that's how come we dream of these people.

I myself *Hanbleceya* sittin there, second night I believe, an uncle of mine came and I shouldn't mention their names but they wouldn't mind. Uncle and my Dad and two of my grandmas came. My Dad stood so far and the Grandmas they come a little bit closer. Where I was sittin' it's a hill and there were crosses there. I know there are no crosses but each *Hocoka* as they call it *Owanka* the altar they build you, there is a cross there. You died there and when they open that, tobacco ties or whatever, that prayer you are suppose to be a new person, old things are gone but new things come.

This uncle of mine he sticks his hand in back of me all way through and he said, "Ah, think nothing of it. I made him," he said. He meant me, "I create him." But that hand came out of the chest, all way out. Soon after that, years later, I had open-heart surgery and Dad stood there and smiled. I didn't have no cigarettes but there was seven cigarettes. I didn't know what that meant. The seven sacred rites I guess. I had to learn. I wasn't given no chance like other people. I said, I'm going to Sundance one day and give *Wopila*, thank you. And that's been since then, been a long time. And there's a lady that sang and how could this woman be singing to me? She sings to me now in the Sweatlodge or wherever. The first time I thought it was sister Emily singing, but at that time it used her. They didn't use blades to pierce me, they used cherry sticks and Leonard is the only person that touched me at that time. Now one grandson, does that. All those things that happen on that little hill it came to reality.

In that whole *Hocoka,* they call people the altar, all the things that are in there, it wasn't there when I got there. It was just the skull and the few *Cannunpa*. But now there is a big altar there. Now people have brought us these Buffalo robes we have, but the skull itself it was left there for me to use, to take care of it. Then another skull came in and that was brought from a young man. He may be having wrong thoughts and this and that but he brought something. He prayed with it and he left it there. So there are two Buffalo robes there, he and she. Two Buffalo skulls, he and she. The staffs and the Bear rug, the Antelope, maybe not the Antelope, the Elk, the Bear, the Horse, they are all there on that altar and they cannot be changed.

When I am gone the next one will take over and Grandma can, the other part is hers, it 50/50 there. They call it role model cause she can't take this and give it away. She'll divide that altar. She'll divide it and you can't do that, you got to keep it together until the day death do us part it says. Then if her daughter, one of them going to inherit that she must have a husband to inherit mine. When I am gone my son takes over and if he has a wife she inherits then. That *Hocoka*, the altar must continue to go. In between that, we can't give this away or not suppose to do that. So I am holding that together as long as I can. And right now all that stuff is in my room next to me. I am trying to hold a family together. If I can do that I can hold other people, help them with their prayers. This is what that woman came to tell the chiefs. You are role model. Sure, he has many wives but they all have something to do. Don't have time to sleep with her, maybe one, the rest, they got to do their work. This is where some of them come along and say Indian Chief has many wives. They say the Mormon's have many wives. I never knew, I never met any Mormon that has many wives. Maybe they do,

I don't know. That is their business. And I respect all women. And that *Cannunpa*, Grandma can have it, she has one. And she has a traveling *Cannunpa*. Maybe it's in here with us or at home. It should be in here at all times, in little handbag. Keep it in vehicle. Only thing I have is sweet grass here. It keep's reminding me of the power and prayers and all that sort of thing.

But Grandma used to have a problem every month. She claimed the moon and I don't get to claim it but now that's over with. She can make my medicine. She can keep my medicine or she can go into my room, fix my prayer cloth and pray for good not pray for bad medicine. Pray for those who have misused you because they don't know. One day they will know. You will be abused, you will be neglected but there is spring coming up. It is spring now.

In about a month there will be phone calls coming in. All they talk about is *Hanbleceya*. They go to the original way; nobody will approach me if we go the proper way. *Hanbleceya* is seven days. Three days you go out in the wilderness, pray, you walk, no drink, no sleep, no eat and you find that medicine. And that medicine you use that in your *Owanka* they call it, your altar. And four days, three days you pray and you give thanks and everything and anything you pray for you get. The fourth day you give thanks and the Morning Star comes, daybreak you come out of there and you go to Sweat-lodge and wipe yourself, smudge yourself and the Sun comes up, you stand facing the Sun and give thanks. That's the true *Hanbleceya*.

In Christianity, Jesus did it 40 days, I believe. Now He made it easy for everyone, all nations. He only give us seven days. Everything is seven. So you know they can't tell me they go overnight or two nights *Hanbleceya* and come out and say I had this vision, I had this dream. Ahh, then you go to a Sundance. If it is meant for you to Sundance something terrible happen and it's all corrected. So you go there and you give thanks and you dance with the Sun. Sun God. God is God. Star God, He is the Star, the Universe, He created all things. So you give thanks. It takes years try to understand, study the Lakota religion. Lakota Way. It's hard to walk this way of life. We are born with it. We live in it. But now it's modern times. Like me talking to this tape.

Sundance, no fire pits, if they have those little gas stoves bring them, use 'em. There will be one place to cook. A group of people want to cook. One day that's theirs. Another group wants to, so be it. All these years maybe we'll get a bunch of people in a group and become family. A mistake happens or you make a mistake or a fault but you try to balance that. If that little feller sits on your right on your left and keeps at it, instigates and before you know it you fall right into it and the other comes along a slaps you along the side of the head. What's wrong with your brain? Right there you can recover and the Spirits are gonna try to see if that love is there. Lakota way, you never brag, what you give is going under the bridge. You don't go around sounding your alms as they call it. Like they say I help Jim, grandfather, $300 this year. I don't know. I didn't say, they said it.

Well, this year I help Grandfather out a $1,000. My goodness, what's gonna happen next year? Two or three thousand? Instead of going up you be going down. That's why I asked if you are a bachelor? I should have said the other way. See you have nothing to worry about. Your mind is somewhere in the future. Many people out there wish they have that. They go along but they got short, I call it stake rope, like puppy out here. Somebody tied it too short and there's one a little longer so they can only go so far and they have to give an account. The only account you can give is to Uncle Sam, I guess. How much tax money? Even here I always tell them get a receipt, give a piece of board, stick a nail in it, put those receipts like that up there. At the end of a year, January, when it snow and cold, go over those receipts. See how much you spend on food, electricity bill, phone bill and say this year I'm going to budget. I'm going to watch the budget real close. Don't forget the church. Somebody said, I must give $108. Did God, did He give $108? He give us all of it. This is Christian talk, but you think I'm talking to you, but it's talking to somebody else. I'm using you, and really at my age I don't have to give an account to anybody only to *Tunkasila* and, in fact, I don't have to cause He already know my thoughts, my plans, some you be surprised.

I use it like this, go this route. Supposing I go to the casino, throw a two-dollar token and what if I get a *Wopila* blessing, hit $5,000, or $10,000, whatever, and I give the Mrs. maybe a $1,000 or $500 she really be tickled. I tell her go flea market or go yard selling. Give one of the boys a couple three hundred, get a motel and take Mom over here. And myself, maybe I'll pick up a young girl. Come on girl, drive for me. My clothing, no, let's just take me over here and give her some money to buy her clothes. And that's that guy he's putting all that in, so he say *Tunkasila* forgive me for thinking that way.

This Earth has many holds. The walls have ears. So you never know what's in the person's mind and somehow it'll work, it'll come to her and it's gonna try to work through her and if she's weak it'll work through Florine then she'll say let it go, give it up, quit, let the young ones take over. If that don't work it'll go to the next person, my kids each one, and if that don't work it'll go to the grandchildren, *Takoja*, and if that don't work it'll go to the boys wives or the girls husbands, if they have any, and if that don't work it'll go to the friends and those friends later. I can't use that one because that's between them and the Great Spirit, why these things happen to them. Maybe that's His way of talking. He says I can't go in because I'm scared, I have heart trouble. Why are they scared of me? So you look at it, these are brothers, and they're my friends. All they do is walk in, sit down, have a cup of coffee with me, smoke the *Cannunpa* or make plans for the future. What's there in Christianity? Even Judas betrayed the Master for 30 silver, I believe, and he hung himself and yet he did that for a purpose. At the end, in Spirit, he will be standing with the Master because he was used, to show that he loved him and he yield himself to him. So he's used. St. Peter denied him 3 times, three or four o'clock in the morning. I don't know him. Here I stand. I used to deny him. I denied *Tunkasila.* Now I don't.

Wherever I go people know what I am, who I am. I love people. I talked to that waitress in that restaurant, I never see her before in my life. And she went along. She said, "Old boy pack up." And she fall right in it, we joke, we had fun. If that's bad then I'm sorry, ya know? To make her smile and joke with me. There's one girl in the back she playing this, how you play the cards. I have already played many times in my life. But those who follow me sooner or later they're gonna give up, but if they go with me all the way they'll have a beautiful future in Spirit world.

Your concerns are here on Planet Earth right now. We argue about this and that, and that shouldn't happen.

Now on this day, look at now. Who have I argued with? Who have I said anything wrong or did I do some gossip? Before midnight I'll have to say I'm sorry not to that person but to the one with the authority. Give me the strength and courage not to ever do that again. That's just the way it is and that's the Lakota way, the way of life I found. I can instigate into some names and I can put that person way down here and if you don't be careful you gonna come right down in your true self and it's gonna come into the open. What kinda person and who you are. Next day you say my friend you be careful. If we don't,

Your concerns are here on Planet Earth right now.

you start gossip, you talk about other things and before you know you gonna start on your husband. If that don't work you gonna start on your own kids, start condemn your own children, your own grandchildren. You're gonna talk about them. Just imagine this happening coming from you. So while that baby was inside of you whatever happens in the future that was you, you plant it there. While that baby was inside of you, you should have talked to it. This time tonight sing lullaby song. While it's in there you talk about good things. When that person comes out, that future there it is already to start good life. But drug and alcohol, gossip and all that when that baby comes out in the future that's your life, that's your creation. Nobody did it, only you. So we gotta be careful.

This is first time I think you have sat and relaxed and enjoyed us. That granddaughter, she's suppose to slow down. She calls me, "take it easy", talkin' about herself. Someone has to practice what they preach. You're not ever going to see you three women sit in this position again. Maybe someday you say, early in spring, snow and all that and remember this morning. I say you'll never see this day again. Tomorrow it's going to be different. It's going to be spotty and next day probably be bone dry. So we've got to take these and teach our young ones, instead, some people they get mad and the evil is in them, in their heart and their mind and that's the one, the Lakota never did have that. They didn't know anything about negative thing, everything positive. They go to bed with the sun when it goes down, then they're up. They don't run themselves ragged, here, there and everywhere. The people that are trying to communicate are the Spirit who is trying to communicate. But the evil can take you. Running back and forth, doing this and that. So we have got to settle down as elders and get it together.

This White Buffalo before I went there was a lot of talk in Indian Country Lakota Times. One young man he said, "This is a sacred thing, it is best to kill it and give the meat to elders and take the hide and put it on top of the hill." Now, what if they say this thing of children, a young girl of his, kill her, skin her and put her on top of the hill and give the carcass to the animal if they'll take it or if he has a sister or his mother. And if they called him a holy man, the papers put it as holy man. I was there and I saw what happened. No one cannot follow me as they did last year. I stood there alone. Where are all my friends? Where is that love? They said they loved me. That nephew is only one. He come up now and then. The rest of them, nobody there. But when I did move they all moved and that's what happened at Buffalo pasture. I walked in barefooted, two Buffalo's danced, the man said, those are her sisters singing as they are dancing. I said that Buffalo is going to change color. And the same young medicine man or holy man or spiritual leader he copied.

Now I said, if it's truly the one, it's going to go back to it's natural color again, the white. It'll never happen cause older it gets it's going to be that color, gray *Pte San Wi*. And they're out there. So always look at this. But maybe this, in some way, is Jesus Christ or our brothers and sisters, since God created all things. And that's the way of the Lakota.

The Universe is a part of that.
There's music there.

You say *Mitaku Oyasin*, we are all relatives, God created all. Everything is our brothers and sisters. Do you talk to these relatives? Do you hear what the wind says to you? Go sit under a tree in the woods and listen. Find out you know nothing. Maybe the stars teach you something. How do you treat your relatives? Thank you for that water, that beauty. Maybe throw McDonalds or cigarette at mother. Run over on the road, that animal, that's your brother. This come back! Respect, honor all that God created. The Universe is a part of that. There's music there.

Important, my great-great-grandfather brought over the holy bible, *Wowapi Wakan,* they call it and *Maza Wakan,* the rifle, *Mni Wakan,* the firewater or Holy Water as they call it, and *I Wakan,* the mouth that can be used to hurt people, the mouth is *Wakan.* These four destroyed this country, nearly destroyed. Look what's happening now. They treat one another like animals and Lakota don't do these things.

So what you hear on TV or radio or papers now there's violence, there's racist, there's prejudice. People are angry at themselves so they try to take it out on other people and it's too bad it has to be like that. Now you have seen the change in them. Curley, his grandfather, is a *Wasicu.* And his mother is half. She try to talk to those people last year. They're funny, she cover that fireplace.

And yet some of these people went on ahead and did their thing. Now they are paying for it. Maybe they did it without a power or whatever.

That one, I feel bad about him using two canes. Some I can say anything I want to him. I think he's big enough to carry it. If he was a patient guy, I'm patient. Maybe something good might happen. But right now he's scared himself. I get scared sometimes. I make a mistake here and there maybe. I sit here at this window. We talk. He plays that pow wow music or church music or Native American peyote song. I enjoy that. It's honor to be with him. Even sit in the Sweatlodge cause some day he leaves, he said. Maybe no regret and through love he says, "I can imagine Dad and take him home." He says, "I found that out."

And I know that he has been neglect and abused and he is just a reminder. But he come a long ways. Like he said, "Tomorrow I'll come check." So he'll be here tomorrow morning. He'll make sure I'll get to the road, if I'm going. If I stay he'll be here at noon hour again. Really check-in and out, really call. He said I don't want to be in the way cause you guys maybe do some recording, whatever. He likes to watch TV. He sits here till midnight then he goes to bed and bead all day. Just like that scanner I have in there. That don't bother me. I know what's going on. Sometimes I have my radio on. Listen to talk show from Denver, Colorado. It don't bother me. I still sleep, I still get up, I get my six hours sleep. That's plenty. If it's four hours then so be it. Every night I deal with pain. Nobody know. You go wherever you want, do whatever you want, say whatever you want. You have pleasure, whatever. I get up in the morning I think about the next day. I know what's going to happen tomorrow. If I don't, it doesn't get, done.

I'm concern about one of the women for a little bit. Her mom wanted too much attention. She give her too much attention. Some people, that's all they want. They take, they take, they take. The more you pray for them the more they take. It's all up there. So when I get in that vehicle down the road sometimes I don't talk. If I have nothing to say I'm thinking what mischief, what words can I use to scatter people, keep them away from me. Sometimes Florine sees the evil or whatever, I don't see it. I can't find the answer. We're going down the road, sittin staring into space, Sundance, they ask me a question when I'm thinking, when I'm talking may be interfering with something that maybe you shouldn't. My minds way beyond.

Wherever I'm going, we're going. We'll get there. I feel like let Him do the talking cause if I talk I'll probably gossip. Talk about people that they're no good and some are good. It's better to let the Spirits talk. Open that door. They can't open that door. I have to open that door inside. The door knob is inside of me. So you can come out, come out, come out and play a million dollars this year. He may not even come out. Might say thank you, or I might not even say thank you. Probably smile, I would say.

I wonder what the hell I'm going to do with all this because you gonna have people come from all over the country. Insurance, mine is cheaper, heart companies be standing all around, religion. You have so many friends you won't be able to tell those people. You'll have a problem there. But from here is nice. I don't have nothing. I take that back. I have that little altar. What's there, I'm trying to keep it together, the family.

I have my little machine that sits here and I play that. It relaxes me. Like this T.V. thing going on and on. If I wanna see the weather or news I turn it to this one. While one ear is listening the other one is thinking, this is where they talk about the left and right brain, I guess. Now bring it together and try to use these back here, far as I can think back. So-called memory block, I guess. And there are some days I don't remember, some years I don't remember, people I met. My age it is really something. If I want to I can go to this one, listen to the sports in a hurry and then I'll go to this one and that's blank but I go to the next one and so it's all there. Next five days I want to hear that I turned to this one and there's nothing there.

One of the grand kids was on that computer. They ask him which keys did you touch. So he touched this and that and this one. "I touched these," he said. This time he added few more. They should have stopped right there and instead they hold his finger to find out. They asked him again. This is this that I touched. He went like that and took off. That was it. Like computer that has that little machine sound, ya' know? That was it. They called him, "Come back junior." Six, seven years old. That was one time. I said, you can make that computer talk after all. Well, look, people are working with the *Wakinyan*, Thunder Beings or Lighting now. And look at this big thing, it's a battery *Wakangli,* electricity, there's water. We gotta let these young ones speak sometimes, ya' know. They might have something better to say than we have. And I think we are gonna be riding with *Wanagi* through here.

Behind walls, there's all kinds of little ants and trees and all that kind of stuff ya' know. Some might not like me using that word, might call them sober drunk. There's an animal in each and every one of us. I don't care how strong you think you are but sooner or later that anger is in you. More important things are always reminding people of the trees, the air, the water and the wind. Organize, discipline, respect, and humble. And I think Jesus said, "The first will come last and the last will come first." Many want to be seen and want to be heard. What kind of weather are we getting?

We have to learn to appreciate. Some day when I'm going away they're going to need to put up a big pow wow, ya' know. Should be while I'm still kicking so I can see. Last year that ceremony at night many priests weren't there. Just few were there. I saw the ones that were there. Saw some things that others will never see. They missed out on that. Even Grandma, she said that, "This is first time I see something." My son says, "I can't believe these things. I don't know about this. He's my dad, my father, but I call him the old man sometimes. I call him *Tunkasila*."

It takes a while, ya' know. And I think all these people make mistake. What do you need, ya' know? What do you want? Then they can't afford it and then they can't come up with it. Like today if someone says what do you need, I'll say I need a pick-up and lumber so I can finish my *Oyate Tahocoka*, Sundance Arbor, out there. They figure I'll say give me a package of cigarette or MacDonald or something, ya' know. Sweet grass maybe. *Otaya,* He already has it all. Most of those people all use to work. Now they're gray and a bunch of those, most of 'em, all walk like babies. And you know, they might not be the oldest there.

That's really bad, ya' know. You look for some elders to ask for advice and they're not there. We'll never see this day again with all this beautiful snow and first thing coming to your mind is gettin' stuck. I can't leave the car on the road. Somebody might this and that.

There is some ladies start making gourds, taking gourds in the Sweatlodge, and drumming. That's not Lakota way. The only person that Spiritual gourd is for is a man. Used to have a Grandma near. She's maybe 80? She use to hold ceremonies. She took all the shoes and placed in front of the door. This is supposed to be Holy ground. What are we doing with our shoes on? Not only here but also wherever we walk. I take my shoes off and walk around here people gonna say, hey, careful you gonna catch cold or say he's crazy. Last time I had on underwear was probably 30, 40 years ago. Can't wear gloves, can't wear cap, hat. It's Sacred.

Hmm, hmm, hmm, hmm. This is something I am trying to understand. About two weeks ago I came to, maybe last winter, ahh, I guess I was thinking about fire. It was told that the Universe was there and all of a sudden there's a thaw of the ice, then fire. How it got up here nobody knows. No one will ever know. There must be another planet out there in the Universe. We're part of that Universe, ya' know. And we talk about the World.

What world are we talking about? We know there is planet Earth. We're here. And then He said, I am the Morning Star in the Evening and then the Sun and He took the moon, and half-moon. When it's a new moon there is a young lady sitting there. Ah when the moon is full you look up there, Grandmother always tell me that, you'll see that pretty lady sitting there with the white dress on. You look at it and ya' know it's like cloud and the moon. Truly it is a lady! She takes flight to earth and there Mother Earth. The women, especially during full moon, time to respect yourself, act like one. There are some do's and don'ts, things to say and things not to say.

You women, don't be lazy, get up and greet that Morning Star. At least once a month give that, *Wopila*, a little water. Every morning, first thing, drink a little water. Water is Life. Put that water on your face and put a smile there. This is a prayer, and honoring. Maybe, for this, He will call you granddaughter, sister or mother.

What you see in that water, that mirror, that's the way you are. You think crappy thoughts you will be crappy. If you say the weather is beautiful, no matter what, then that's the way you are. These thoughts, you control, that's the way. The world that's you.

We have to learn to appreciate.

I always thought about that. That volcano they were talking about. That's the beginning of time. *Wakinyan* came up and made the shape like a *Cannunpa.* That smoke come out, ya' know. Just picture it in your mind. From that center point comes out a diamond shape, in the middle of one side there's a woman, one side a man. In Christianity this man they call Jesus Christ and the other side the lady is the Lakota Woman, the Calf Woman. They say Calf Woman or the Buffalo Woman or, whatever, that brought the *Cannunpa.* And there's rules there, laws She shared and in Christianity. At the tip of the diamond, all around, ahh gee, I don't know what they call it, like a star, ya' know. Little tiny stars certain different colors and all that smoke goes back up there. And that's what I don't understand, I mean you are you and me and Him and you. So later I am the only one that talks to my angels. Well, He said that I will not use angels and somehow we use animals for Lakota way. The Spirit of that animal; ants, dinosaur or whatever, those are sisters and brothers.

We talk about Adam or atom but the Buddha nobody talking about. There are some using other people but if not seek himself how does he know there is just the atom? We go into the Sweatlodge ceremony, we see the atom, the shiny little stars in there. You're a living star, I am one, everybody, shining stars. But that little Circle, what would you call that? A little spark like the little lightening bug and when it goes out that means a little evil after your mind or your heart or your body that weakens it, puts out that light. So with all your mind you have to keep it going and make your face to shine upon people with your face, when you smile. You make people, your face has something to do with it too. That's why I always say you get up in the morning with a smile and you go to bed with a smile and tomorrow is another day so your face should be shinier than yesterday.

I'll try to bring this Indian religion, it's so close to *Tunkasila Wakan*, Sacred Grandfather. *Wakan*, the Creator. It is not to play with. Today I was sitting there thinking, ya know? Every church or organization has man made rules and a few by-laws and 50 more. But with me I don't believe in by-laws. In the future, why so be it, ya know? But just as long as I go believing in God and I never claim anything on this planet earth, that's it. I make a mistake once and tried to claim my wife, ha, suppose to be my friend. My children are not mine. They were left to me to teach them the right way to go. Still they learn from other resources. As we go along it's going to be harder.

Ahhh, the story of the rock. I'll never forget his face, never forget his face. That's imprinted up here. It was so funny. I don't know, last year remember I was sitting in that chair, after he came back that way, I had him bring in that rock, that hot rock from that fire pit and he handed it to me and someone gave me a towel and that towel burned and how this kid believed. He carried that rock in and it never burned, but it burned the towel.

Those rocks are Sacred, gathering ask permission, your mind must be clear so you don't put negative on there. Make sure those are new like baby or virgin, never used. They hear, help set thing straight, forgiveness in that. Always give *Wopila*, thanks. These are the ancestors.

Now, why these things happen, ya know? I was sicker than a dog. When I got to the clinic, the hospital, I was alright, there was nothin wrong with me. But they had to keep me overnight. Many times I learn a lot being in the hospital. Maybe that's one way of Him talking to me.

After that was over, then they thought surgery, heart surgery and still the records were there. They thought that was impossible that a man in that condition they just didn't cut me off. They thought I was some kind of people, person to go through all that. But you take care of yourself, you know? You work with the doctor.

I couldn't find a medicine man to help me but I went to the *Wacasa Wakan*, the Holy White Man, the doctor. And he helped me. Two weeks later I went back and both my legs were healed. But I don't know what made me sick to my stomach at that time. Maybe so many people there and everybody had an idea of this and that, but they forgot one thing.

They were concerned, they prayed, *Wocekiye* and still something happened, ya'know? Much before that I had ulcers, diabetes, gallstones, arthritis and all that and only thing I live with now is diabetes. The other day took my own blood test, 133. If I keep it there I'll feel good, ya' know? It get lower than that it makes me sick, weak. So maybe somebody likes me. I don't know. My luck in here, I'll probably be the last one.

Though some evangelist's with a name, always negative, threatening people, everybody's goin to hell. That's somethin' I wasn't taught. In that book over there reading and standing there, it says why Christ passed over. I've been there, ya know? The last name I carry is sort of destruction, ya know? It seems like out here, ya know, but it's the name I'm stuck with. I have an uncle out here with a good name. He's sort of my role model, he's 90 some years old. And his wife, I think there's some 70 years of marriage. I have good teachers out there. Never been scolded by any of them. When they come for me they never talk about drug and alcohol and womanizing or manizing or whatever they call it. He knows I have 16 wives, ya know? Had a probate and she inherited all the kids. They give her everything and that's the ones she gave back.

In back of it the new Sundance land, the superintendent he's just a friend, really a cousin and he said I want to help all I can. So they are giving another section back there in the hills where the people can *Hanbleceya* and so forth. I said, "I want a playground for young people." She never forgot that. West of the grounds, that's where the playground will be. But someone has to see it through. I'll try.

I was once told, you will have new land. I said I never claim anything or I don't ask except one time. I told one of my angels I need thousand bucks. Within the week, a thousand bucks. Gee, if I can ask for that much every day would they give it to me, ya know? There is a lot of work to be done. My angels, they've just started. A couple of them tried to get married but it didn't work. Find a rancher, a farmer, or a big twin towers, but it seems like it don't work. Right after people leave Bill, uncle Bill started writing or else letters. He's a mean guy ya know, Bill? Whenever you don't pay your bills why Uncle Bill says, "I ask you in a nice way and I give you two weeks and if not electricity goes out and there you are. We struggle. Someone figured out last year, if everybody who showed up, if only 300 people showed up and everybody gave $20, that's all, that is $6,000. Wow, I feel like a millionaire.

Four hundred eighty five families there last year. Sitting out there with people and you know people are sitting in there running that TV, ya know? And it's like I come in that Lincoln. That never got to us, ya know? Just imagine how many people use that shower they taking and so far they burned out one or two stoves, how many coffee pots? You just got to keep going, ya know? Like some understand but what about the rest. They are looking for something out there. They want an easy way.

That one knows about the brain, right and left brain and how many veins in that brain and all the colors in that brain and when they start saying "they said," I keep thinking about those things she's talking about. Buddhist, I saw a Buddhist dance, monk or whatever they are. Boy, they are good dancers. He dressed like a woman with all those wraps, he was dancing with the women. But that lady, oh, she had a pretty voice, maybe, someday. She didn't know no other song in Lakota. That was honest you know. This is what we are trying to do, how can we make this world,

> **God's Spirit can talk to you through your brain not through your ear.**

earth beautiful? Border to border, coast to coast. Trees and all. It just hit her, America the Beautiful, America or whatever that song. Maybe some others did understand.

Ah, 500 veins, I don't know everything there is to know about the brain, only *Tunkasila*. I know it has trillions and trillions of connections. Spirit can talk to you, God's Spirit can talk to you, through your brain not through your ear. So that means this part here on top must be sort of a soft spot somewhere that connects with Spirit, in and out. They say where baby's soft spot is, is where the Spirit comes in and where it leaves. That's what I heard and some went to school for that.

It's time to sing a song. The Four Directions song, those words: *Wiohpeyata etun wan yo! Nee tunkasila Ahitunwan yankelo. Che ke i yo! Che ke i yo! Ahitun wan yanelo.* That's to the West, Grandfather it's me , I am sitting there waiting, look here! Pray to Him because He is looking at you!

Then there are those others; *Waziya takiya*, north; *Wiohiyanpa*, east; *Itokaga* , south; *Wakatakiya* , above; *Wakantanka,* Holy Spirit; *Maka takiya*, down at Earth, your Mother; *Nikunsikun*, Grandmother. These you pray to, say *pilamayaye*,or *pilamaya yelo* always get answer.

By Sundance time when they sing, people should all sing, instead of standing around, prancing around, bouncing all over. One year we couldn't get it up, it was a big tree. Last few years it's been kinda small, ya know. We use to have a great big tree. That first time we came back from Kyle, Fool's Crow took my right hand and he lift it and he said, "Say this facing West." and I said it after him and I finished. I love to hear that tree talking. It was a *Hanbleceya* song but they made it into a Sundance song. They know me, ya know. So all those songs they are singing is about me. I love the hospital so much that I recovered and I come back later.

It's not that we try to create a god or I'm trying to create a god in my image, me, but I let the Spirit work through me. Many times when things get hard I sing a song in the Sweatlodge, ya know. When it's time for the Spirit to come or whatever or when I present myself to the Great Spirit. And *kola* means friend. He is my friend. I think this is kinda bad because I'm loud and many times the Spirit comes to me and I don't need a mike.

One time in Denver, I was at blessing grounds and I stood there and I sang and next day I notice they set up drum and 10 or 12 people sitting around the drum and they still didn't use that mike. One of the boys said, "You know last night my dad," he says, " he sang all by himself and we could hear him all over and look at us we have to use a mike. Gee, we don't have no voice."

67

But then I use to have a voice, but now Spirits got that, but anyway listen up, everything goes with the song. Let's be patient. I want to go the time, at the beginning of time while this Lakota's still crazy. To get into the Sundance all these things come in line, ya know, like chain of command. What to do, next step and next step. And I think that's gonna be good. A lot of these people are people they don't know. There are medicine men out there they don't know. They call themselves this, they even call themselves a holy man and to me I don't think this. We'll go step-by-step on these things here.

Take a pencil and draw a Circle when it comes to the end, is there an end or does that Circle just keep going? That Circle keeps going. There's no end. There's beginning but there's no end. There has to be a beginning, *Tunkasila*. So what would you call that? The Circle of Life? I'm trying to work on a title for the book. That sounds good, Circle of Life. Beginning , no end.

At the beginning of time, that's my time, there is the Circle and there's no end. As I travel the Circle the people start coming in, into the Circle with me, from all directions. From outside you can come in but you can't go out, only the thief can come in and the thief will go out. It's given that, like Christ and His disciples. *Tunkasila*, He picked. God has touched one that betrayed Him, he came into the fold, the Circle with a few silvers, whatever, he snuck out and betrayed Him. There are people that have already betrayed me. Ever since I started they come and go but the Circle of life itself has no end, there's no death. Death means sleep. Today they were talking about death like there's no more, but death means sleep, your body sleeps but the Spirit lives on. This is a Circle, that's the thing I'm talking about.

That Granddaughter said, "Come and visit me, okay?" So I go and visit her. Tomorrow we're going to someplace about an Earth Center. I got to thinking; I thought South Dakota was the center of the earth, scientists and whatever, say this. Oh, well. Okay. And she never tells me anything. Then I see the people coming in, you know? Hey, wait a minute. What's this? I see a minister with a Bible came in, storybook or whatever. I think he was just there to judge me or see if there was love to come out of my mouth. Later, he admits, and he becomes my friend. I saw him somewhere way beyond before I ever met him, I mean physically. I saw his picture with the loaf of bread, the bread of life. Somewheres I don't know where. There's bunch of books, pamphlets. It has tuition $67. Wait a minute I said, all these people, each one payin' $67 just to hear me. Gee, I'm a cheapy guy I guess. I didn't know anything about the money, it's not the Lakota way. All in all, I was supposed to visit her. And the next year, oh boy, it could have went up $100 I believe. Oh, gee. It kinda caught on. I thought $600, that was nice. And the third trip or fourth.

Remember it blizzard? And before I knew it a man and a woman was arguing, Hey, wait a minute. Why are these two arguing? Later the man took off. So I figure, no more of this, ya know? That's the time , my daughter, tied the muffler with a shoestring and it didn't burn. That sure could have burned. I had that money in my pocket and I went to a hall that evening. Bunch of money.

I never asked for any money. Someone set it up and I was blaming that granddaughter for that, but she not know, later I found out after I had that ceremony in that huge building. Instead of helping we might have hurt this center cause every week or every other week they had someone there talk, talk, talking, drum singing, or drum making or whatever. To me I am sorry about that, upset the fruit basket.

I didn't understand when they said, during that blizzard, no one can go out or come in, okay, and here that friend of mine he took off with one of the angel's and brought her mom back and nobody could come back, go out or in. We're really funny people, huh? And I get telephone number, I forgot someone gave me a telephone number. I forgot someone said that one of the boys called and he said, "That if you can't get out a copter will come, then pick up your car tomorrow and you'll be on your way." Somehow he's on the road. Either they went wrong or I went wrong. Something happened, so everybody did good. But we must forgive, but never forget and never do it again.

I looked at all those people and said, "How many of you are coming to Sundance?" That granddaughter said, "Oh, no!" And then I turned around and said, "You're responsible for every mistake they make."

That one, the first time I saw him, he was sitting, remember? I said King David, and his name was like that, and that he called his little one over. Oh, he was proud. That's my daughter. He didn't know I was going to say anymore, he didn't know he was going to haul wood for a couple of years. I will not call you this and that. I will call you Mom and Dad. This is from my people.

That baby girl, would you come? That Little One and I, we have work to do. I said, "Forget about that fawn." I prayed and prayed. She wrote a beautiful little thing there. I'll always treasure that. Maybe few words and listen careful to every word. This is where I'm at and listen careful and do likewise. You're with us and

you work in your way. You'll sing, bringing the words, the message, okay? Let your mind, your heart, okay? Sing "Amazing Grace". All this is glory happening. In Lakota, he prayed and he prayed and finally he sang, that's how it happened. *Tunkasila, Tunka heyla, chee-wah–kee-yelo.* And that's what he sang, he says, I'll pray to God and then everything else will happen. And every day, especially today, I guess, many places has those songs, but in English and Lakota. I hear but I don't know the way, He said, as it goes,
Almighty God, made a way for me.
Wanikiya, as they call Him.

When a woman's a grand-mother, she can drum, but just socially.
Never in the lodge. Others try, I don't know, but Lakota way doesn't do that. You take Choctaw, Hippie, Cherokee or whatever, they can drum and rattle inside the Sweatlodge as long as they use their own language. Don't use the Lakota language or a song that's sung by the Lakota. Lakota women, *Winyan,* don't take rattles. *Yuwipi* man, that rattle, it comes to them. They have to make their own and make their own drum and then truly use their own language. If a Woman is sittin' there, and a man walks in, *Tunkasila,* here that woman says, "huh, what's going on?"

If a woman's running that lodge and you pray you should say "Grandmother, tell Grandfather." So you go *Unci, Tunkasila, Unci*, tell him.

I don't care how you pray, whoever prays with that *Cannunpa*, that's the Lakota way and the power is right there. The Lakota, the tongue, the brain, the heart all speak Lakota. If you're going to use Lakota words in the Sweatlodge then you say, *Tunkasila,* forgive for all these things and *Mitaku Oyasin* and sing *Wiohpeyata.* Wait a minute. You become a shaman then, imitator. That's what it's all about. That's what it means.

No offense, other tribes I don't know or care what they do as long as they use their own language. They can beat that drum as much as they want to, and do all the rattling they want. But the only one thing I hear is a man. I was shown a gourd, this man he said, "Look at it, hold it." When they open the flap this is the gourd, but now it's like a dipper, that was a gourd one time.

That's the gourd. It's not made out of skin. That might be your skin or your head you're holding, rattling in there, your own, unless it's given to you. The Spirit, like Bear Butte, did this. I still have that gourd. That gourd, I never used it, but that gourd I had Aztecs pray with it. I said pray, pray, pray till it works. Four things he prayed in the second round. He had that gourd sittin' there. Now he will remember always. And that came from the North. And brother, Tony Mandan, he says,

"Albino, from the south, come on in." I figured that's when I met my White Buffalo, my Elk, my Bear. I already met, the Eagle, and the Thunder scratched my back. I always knew they had to cover me I guess. I had nothing to be shame of, nothing to hide.

So this other brother, if he can I can, he was undressing and some woman hollered, "Hey, Indian, shame on ya." How come they saw him and didn't see me? And that brother he is in terrible pain. All he had to do was to forget, that went under the bridge. He did some things, that's good. That mistake, never do it again, but be a teacher. Tell others not to do it. My life is everyday, this is my way of life. All this, it may not work. Who knows?

Time has broken that machine, that tape recorder. Someone should have remind me. Maybe that should have been wrapped with the sage. Maybe a tie, prayer cloth. Then it might work. So what you do is you pray about it. Be honest to yourself. Be honest to everybody. This is maybe meant for a purpose. That's my way of life. When your prayers are answered must honor Spirit by *Wopila.* Sometimes tobacco, flesh, suffering is enough, but whatever Spirit asks you must give, even you life. Not do this and someone must suffer for you, sometimes those that love you.

And I love people. I have four boys and four girls. I love them very much. And they are still with me. One I worry about, but he is old enough, I guess, to take care of himself, maybe his son will take care of him. When that Sweatlodge is open, even though I'm weak I go in. I never forget. So that's my life. Now there's someone wants to make *Wopila*. Maybe there's a purpose for it. All she has to do is thank that man that prays for the baby, and the people that are concerned about the baby's heart. That's why that hole is there, healing. Now the other one's working on it. That heart will be whole. Now, like I told her, this summer we all have to say *Wopila*, thank you, for giving that child a future. We offer gifts to those who pray for that heart, and advise him as he go along. This is the year of the children. Every year they say that, but we never give them nothin real.

Last year that *Hanbleceya* was a good one, nine of them went out. I said to my son, take care of them. He does ceremony. Tony Mandon he came out. Start talking Italian and laughing. I hear some of those words, and I started growing tall. He got scared. I went back in the tipi, I thought, I heard these women, they're out there. Near the Sweatlodge I heard all these women, two hours they're out there. They all came down. Only Beetle-juice was here, tinkerbell was here and her little puppy.

75

So that's what they seen was that little puppy and that woman going by. Steve had that old medicine bag. I could get one of the Grandmas, she was snoring. He said, "Every chance she could get she would make the sound of snoring." But one year we had 87 up there at one time and that's too much.

Well, like I told you, you want to live so be it. You want to die? You die alone, but if you want to live we'll always be together. There is some things you can do and some things you can't. Save yourself a little bit. People are there to enjoy and you can enjoy them.

A week before that, one of my toes was purple. When I got there, that hospital, my ankle was purple, I had gangrene. A doctor came from Pennsylvania, told them to take me in right away, so they did. And the Rapid City doctor said, "Quick, gangrene has set in." And then the next doctor came in and said, "Mr. Dubray, what do you want us to do?" Because he probably thought just to cut it off, ya know? My doctor said, "What you want us to do? Chop it off?" I said "Doctor save that little trouble for me." Three days later that purple was gone, all of that gangrene was gone.

That doctor said, "Be careful do not drink this." First thing they did was bring me that. I don't know who brought me that, it was orange juice but the other kind. I thought who'd want to kill me that night. I didn't have the courage or strength to come and go, you know. There is an elderly guy from Wyoming who kept hollering, "Shirley, help me." I guess Shirley was his wife, who had died 36 years ago. But he kept hollering, "Tell those doctors, at least you listen to me. Nobody will, dam you listen." The doctors, they all came in. "You know," he says, "you doctors and nurses, you three, don't know a hootin' thing, not that way." The next day I was released. That was good though. Then Grandma went in, remember?

When I come out of the hospital, these people help, thinking that they are so *Wakan.* Back at the motel, that's where I really suffered. All the others decided to give me a healing, after the healing, I stood up then fell down. I tell you, these guys were trying to get rid of me. They were all into their egos, I'm gonna fix him and I can do it, but I stood up and fell down. I guess I was as bad as that elderly guy. Somebody help me, anybody. Whatever you need, go to Jesus, go to *Tunkasila,* whatever, They helped me. I thought I gotta get away from these people, but there they were and there and here, all over. What you want? What you need? You wanna eat? Oh, why me? They meant well, I guess.

That's when someone bought all kinds of shoes. Heel, toe, size 13's, pair of shoes, left side. Those shoes tells them. Twenty three pairs, no, it was only four pairs of shoes. Anyhow, they had a whole box full of shoes. I don't know how they do it but they had one that was 9, one 9 1/2, one was 8 1/2, one was size 8. I sent that granddaughter to get shoes and she brought back the wrong size. She went back to get the right size, and she brought them back. One was a size 8 and one was a size 9, so she went back again. She said to Steve, "I'm not coming here again." So she pulled the right size, and they were both left feet. So we went back and Steve is cracking up. Finally, the fourth time she got the right pair of shoes.

Then one of the others went out, "I got to get a pair of shoes for my brother." They tell him that one size is nine and one is eight, or something like that. I believe. So he goes out and gets size nines. Then he kinda looks this way and that way and looks to the left side, then he takes a nine for left foot and right. The other he took an 8 for the right, hee ha, but when he got it back, left one, eight. The third trip he came back with both on the right side, so that didn't work. I was wondering what's going on now. What are these people?

At one time I took off my shirt and the old lady said, "He's Rambo, he's silly or hey." She said, "Cover up that skeleton. Somebody might see you." My gosh! I looked at myself. What happened? Rambo, he's gone.

Before he was gone Robo Cop came along, but there I was and each year I got a little deeper. This past winter I had three or four visions. I said, "I'm not worthy, the last one." Then here comes a turtle shell, that's part of that vision. I said, "I am not worthy." It's too late. I touched it. This evening, the rainbow that was here was part of that. I told the boys some, that *Hocoka,* that altar, I had was all there, the Buffalo skull and all that, the rest of the animals would help me, the Buffalo, the robe, the next one, the cow, the female Buffalo skull, elk, horse, everything there. You people had *Tunkasila* put that altar together, but I said I'm not

Don't judge one another.
Love one another.
Today is gone,
tomorrow is a new day.
It's a beautiful one.

worthy. It's too late. These hands have touched it. Life says get out, but I got in a little deeper because I must walk with my cross, with my *Cannunpa.* I pray He'll give me at least one hour, once a month and I can do what ever I want. He granted me that. I'm still a human being. I was once and now I really know what common is, *Ikce Wicasi.* You can claim all this as mine, mine isn't here. This past year, here, over there, I had a piece of that rock but who cares? The mountain had a piece of it, that's when that *Hocoka* came.

And thanks to my great-grandfather, he only had five wives and probably in every state he had a girlfriend. Now with me, there's *Tunkasila* and my better half. If I said my worse half, I'll be sleeping with *Sunka,* the dog, in the bathroom. It's getting late, so I said my better half. I try, but she kiss me on the cheek. I don't blame her, my lips aren't spongy anymore. Always did have long hair, ponytail, now Shetland ponytail, piggy tail, whatever. All I remember is Samson, the power, the language he gave me. Lakotas, don't understand, English, whatever, nobody understands. I told the little one that second song forget about it, that was me.

I was barely 56 years old when Mother went and as it was going they were taking her. Hey, I said slow down, but I did get part of me there, take it with you, where it came from, I came from you. And I guess at that time people call me Sundance Chief and all that. I was just a little bitty baby boy and I thought it was over, here she comes back through the East and give all her belongings to burn. Spiritually, she took everything. Brothers and sisters, they keep pictures and that's all we have for memory and to teach. Early evenings, she said, that she'd sing a gospel song, Lakota, pitch pine stove, kerosene lamp, stick a potato in the stove. I think that's baked potato. No radio, no television, no nothing. Peaceful, now Spiritually they come. We can't go and they can't go, then one day we will go and there it is.

I was Daddy's little boy, Mama's little boy, but I had to stop. Rest of the brother's were younger than I am, but I am still here and most of them are all gone. I think two are left, they both not doing very good. But I have these people and many, many more and I'm the one that's suppose to tell these things.

Don't judge one another. Love one another. Today is gone, tomorrow is a new day. It's a beautiful one. And always remember somebody made a way for it. And He never said a different one loves me. You, you and you walk with that. And hopefully next time it'll be on outside. We'll make sure that it don't rain. Maybe we'll have a nice huge, we'll have an Indian Holy Ghost time. We'll shout, we'll dance, have now, that's good and say I danced for *Tunkasila*. I danced for my Lord. So this is two that come together. We only serve one God. He is the only God. So while He can, He said, "Let us make man in our image, *Wicasa Wakan*."

At this time maybe have a short prayer, *Wocekiye*, and maybe next time, some time, down the road, I'm to cross this road again, we'll have good time.

Cannunpa Wolakota waye, you walk with that Peace Pipe. You put tobacco in and you inhale it, the tobacco you inhale, you blow it back on the people. They call that smudge. And you give them that medicine from that. Mother Earth comes through that tobacco to you and that's how *Tunkasila* uses it! Just like last night, I sat here and while I was watching boxing, you gals came that way and came back this way and that way. I have a time coming that I will rest, the long rest, but my Spirit will go on. There's no end to death. It goes back to God's energy, we keep on going. Then we will get to inhale all the autumns, atoms, and whatever is out there. But right now we have to do it on our own here. He gave us that chance. We don't dare take anything from Him, try to claim it. Everyday something new comes along, formation of trees, like all that snow. Night before was beautiful icicle and today it snow. If I had a camera I could be taking pictures if she had a camera and somebody took it we would get no pictures. Those are things you put on books like this. Put something on that front page that's life. Circle of Life. All those in there that is good words.

There's life in there but death on the outside. If it's so sacred, Buffalo, why are we eating it? The Buffalo and I, there is no difference. If you can eat the Buffalo, after a while you'll be eating me. When that Buffalo runs out years back you may say something is sacred, today is sacred, every day on that land is sacred. To get on the road and say that road is gonna be bad. We said it, that's what's bad. Common sense didn't come from the book.

You've seen Grandma move. She can save all that movement for another time it'll extend her life. The grand kids may need some advice. One day I'll be sitting here alone if she don't be careful, she'll burn herself out. The only time she rests is when we take those long trips, I guess. Take a vehicle, flying you get there in a hurry, you see nothing, you hear nothing, nothing, you're up in the air. Just trying to be one of the birds. Here, everyday you see something and then you pass through the cities, it changes overnight. It seems like. Hey, what happened to that street? There's a huge overpass over it. And it takes me back to Buck Rogers comic books. Big city there, overpasses like that, and pretty soon there's a globe there.

People live in that globe. You approach a city and you see all that smog, that globe of smog. And they inhale all those atoms that guy was talking about it, that little atom the vehicle that throws out. People pretty soon, after a while, they're going to recycle the water. You go one minute and next minute you be drinking it back. We're talking, it's out here. We say joking, I'm going outside and take fresh air and pollute my lungs. And how can this tobacco cause you cancer when God created all things. He said "It's good," and He blessed it. He said, pray for it. Who are you to condemn God's creation? These are some of the things we have got to think in our hearts and say before it comes out of the tongue. That's why I never say what He created out there is bad. He said, "It's good," and He blessed it. So how can I condemn something that He creates, what I might have created, all I create is problems for someone.

So some of this maybe scientist will say, hey, that drunken Indian don't know nothing. And scientists said there is no God. But before he dies he goes back to that God. There has to be a God. You can create one or go with the real one. One that you can push around, or create something that you can use. I use all things. I can use people's God that they create. I can see if it is truly holy, but some of them they create a stingy God. Just me, me, me all to themselves. The Lakota is given a God that's concerned for all people. What He takes He shares with others. Don't keep it for Himself. So He is struggling, He is suffering.

The other day I was sitting, really suffering, you know? People say they were standing at the cross and the Peace Pipe, *Cannunpa* they call. They're not suffering. They have money in the bank. They have a nice house, that is in their name. Of course, they pay government a little money every month or year, so called tax money. They themselves said Christ cleaned out a tabernacle, the church a house of prayers, not merchandise. This Man that walks with His medicine goes to temple, *Pejuta Ehannamani.* My house, house of worship, not merchandise, one of His helpers says, I will get tobacco smoke. You suffer like I suffer, everything fall on you, carry sins of world. Know when I come, okay, we will smoke in peace. I will leave you with my peace; I will be with you until end.

He said, way before He was born these things are prophecies. He told that one day that they were going to use Him. How much money do people make at Easter time and Christmas? How many of them have made money off of Him? When He was born was there toys, was there wrist watches, diamonds all that stuff? And where did the eggs come from, baby chickens, bunnies? When He was resurrected were all these things there? Thanksgiving time, turkey come in, stuffing, all that, but here on this Turtle

There's no end to death. It goes back to God's energy, we keep on going.

Island they might say it was already here. They use everything from an animal even the bone. There's cattle, there's Buffalo, look at their hooves, the shell comes off. There is a little bone in the shape and they call it *Pte*, Buffalo. Later they say that's a cow, cattle and before long *Pte Wakan*. And these little horses toes or whatever, they take a dog the bone. There's little animals there, horses and just a little puppy. So we already had the toys He gave us. And they already had the football, the basketball, hockey, it's already here in Lakota country, Shinny game, that's just like the hockey. And the goalie is always the woman standing there with her dress, a buckskin dress. You pass, when you get that ball and pass her, you score. It takes a good man. If this game was still going I would use the old lady and that granddaughter. With the two of them standing there, no ball would go through.

So those playing with the world right now, they throw the ball then they start hitting the ball. People come apart but the ball, they don't come apart because that ball is made out of Buffalo hay, Buffalo grass they call it. You help one you help all of them. You feed one you feed all of them. You clothe one you clothe all of them. You abuse one, you abuse all of them, you neglect one, you neglect all of them. Whatever they ask Mama and Daddy, and Mama and if Daddy don't give they go to grandfather. Grandpa, it's like this and Grandpa says give them that, you better give, you don't give you don't inherit nothing, you fall right there. That's the Lakota already practicing, not practicing; he's already in it, in God's power and chain of command. So I guess we don't know everything, huh? What did that preacher say? He stood there, and he said, you don't give me eight million dollars two weeks from now God is going to take me. If I say, "Girls, are you going to get out there and get me $8,000, or God's going to take me." You'll probably all laugh, take him, ha, we don't need him here. And somehow it works, you know?

Last fall, I believe, someone said, they thought about, they thought, their thinking was wrong. It's about gambling. They brought that gambling in, into my life. So nobody really knows me. I go along because few girls say lets go to Deadwood or let's go to Prairie Wind. I'm glad the weather is like this or you would have talked yourself into going. And I would be driving and you would spend three or four hours playing nickels. We got to think, I waste little time. It sure is pretty out there.

Every year I pray that this Sundance we are going to just have seven or eight people. And what happens, all of a sudden you get ninety and go down the line. Half hour or hour say, "good morning, welcome," some, "welcome home." Been a good year, I hope. If it's bad, you made it bad. If it's hard, you made it hard for yourself. But this year I will tell who is going into the Circle and who is not. Who's going to be the teacher out there? Cause many of our young people are going to be leaving the reservation this coming year, this fall. Ahead of time, three or four years, ten years ahead of time this should be warned what to expect out there. Cause there are good things out there, but from that system to ours bad things come in. So they think that's all there is.

Drug and alcohol wasn't here many years ago. It came from the outside into the nation. Now the way they dress, the way they talk, that's not Lakota. Somehow that evil out there got into the Lakota Nation and that could be used right.

She's pouring water, making it rain. Whenever there is a positive, there is always a negative and there are no bad words in Lakota. Whatever your mind thinks you fall right into it and that's the way it will be. They brought it, that pipe, to me so I was sitting there smoking and they accuse me smoking marijuana. They said, no wonder he's out there moving like nothing wrong. I said, only thing he put in there was peppermint. We have peppermint tea don't we? There's always somebody out there. They'll say *Mitaku Oyasin,* they'll go down I guess.

They went to get the tree, came back said that big *Wasicu,* white man, he sent me back out and he pushed that tree down, so I laughed. That same year, no, a couple years later, that one, *Wopila,* he's going to take a cow. I said kill it before you cook it, about 3:00, so the meat can be cured so nobody will have tummy ache. Oh, he was proud. He took a live cow and tied a rope. A bunch of us said we must kill it tomorrow so he tied it. Ahh! *Waste*! He came at 3:00 sharp, that cow choked itself on that rope, it was just laying there. I said remember that. Funny, I told that story. Look what time, it's 3:00. Believe it or not, this one, I mean confidentially, people entertain me.

Hanbleceya time or Sundance time. A lot of fun. I think that son might know some of it. Just tried a couple of weeks ago, we go out there bunch of little kids, some been to Rosebud. They are specialists in the Lakota religion. But thin little ice, just the skin. Good people. Everybody's good. But this is it, when you sit and relax.

Try not to use much wood. The dead wood, the trees down that creek, one thing we'll need is about 8 or 10 pickup trucks to clean that out. There be no cherry, nobody going to chop some sticks there to use. They can take it from other **Sit still and pray.** place, take it in there. No sage will be picked there. Water, they can haul their own, take their own water with them. It's time everybody learned. It's time that people start listening to me. When the Sundancers go in I say people stay away, keep away. Stay in the camp at least till 8:00, 9:00, 10:00. You see that grandma, Lakota woman, and grandpa they sit, they be sitting in chairs and kids go there and they sit. And women I don't know how to tell them, pass the word around, take a blanket, put it down and sit and don't stand up when that *Cannunpa* start coming. Sit still and pray.

In the past, I saw women out there with thin dress on, no bras, bouncing around, swinging their arms. That's no rock-n-roll place to do those things. Women suppose to respect themselves when the *Tanka Wakan* is there, Holy thing, wait until 10:00, 11:00 they come over and sit down. Don't surround with people who just stand there and look at you, at these people, made a commitment, to those people, to pray. Make sure that nobody grabs my shoes and my skirt. I got close to the camp at one time, good thing I had my boxer trunks, they didn't take that. Had my medicine bag here and I walk, souvenir, that's no respect.

We need the Lakota to heal themselves, cause they're concerned, you know. I appreciate all these other people that help. Maybe fourth day everybody go in and give thank you, dance together and pray and say thank you together. Don't ever say, use, the word I Sundance. You're not the sun. The sun is the one that dances with your mind, your heart. Don't lay around and say "I'm tired." To begin with, if you're tired you have no business going in there.

There is no vision quest, *Hanbleceya,* there's no such thing as vision quest. Something happened in the past. You pray and you pray that thing is healed, whatever, you go there and you give thanks, then you have communion with *Tunkasila,* that tree standing there. You go to church and they give you Holy Communion, this is the body of Christ, blood of Christ. I go there, that's true, it's the only thing He give me. I give my bread to Him, my blood to Him, the wine within me, a piece of the living bread. I'm not talking about death, it's the living that we go on. In Lakota way we don't tell these things, it's sacred. We keep it to ourselves. With all the people know the *Cannunpa,* Sweatlodge, *Hanbleceya* and Sundance.

There are seven sacred things that are given to us each. These seven sacred rites, making of relative, keeping and releasing soul, crying for a vision, making of a woman, Sweatlodge, and the others. She brought these to us, teach us to walk this way, the Red Road. These are like Ten Commandments. Today, not just history, at Sundance no one sees when they are done, some see by invitation, wise one. Those that know Spirit, they still do. Those that believe see *Cannunpa,* real power. Seven, seven times seven. So what's seven times seven? Forty-nine? And that seven makes it fifty-six. For fifty-six times seven and from there like a star it goes out there another seven times seven. If you don't know your math, you don't belong there at all.

My grandmother said, you start from the East counting the stars. When you get to the East, Morning Star to Evening Star, your job is done. The old man says, stay away from that Moon, that belongs to the women, that young girl sits there. Half moon, legs hang, straddles her legs, shower her blessing, the blood that flows life. And when the Moon is full, she sits there fully dressed, smiling, and I go out there and with that respect.

I was the only one probably that, that woman came and said I'm going to dance for Mary. Okay, who's Mary? My son was there, I was dying I guess and all a sudden I drank, she gave me prune juice, and my goodness gracious I danced for Mary with my oxygen. I went into the bathroom, cleaned the inside of me, sit there watching the planes come in. But these are sacred, I never tell. There are a lot of things.

That book said good things about me, but the only thing this person make a living off of it and became like that skeleton. Some use me. So this one might come in with a new truck. If he says, "Grandfather I'm going in there," then I'm going to say, "Thank you." I'm going to have to let him go, cause he's the one that brought the thing together. And he has that respect, which he was not, but he wants to be there to see it. And right there, forgive neighbors and other nation. That one found that out. Just because she touched my hand she thought she could Sundance right now.

The first time observe, like your doing. Look and listen. It might take you 10, 15, 20 years and one day you can say it like I do now, you can say, 54 years I've walked with this. I might have made a mistake here and there. I never asked except last October, November, September, I asked. And one of them said, is it gambling? I said no, this is not gambling. I gambled all my life with these people from other places.

There are many jokers that come along, *Iktomi*. They thought they made a monkey shine out of me but they made themselves mockery because they try to mock, mockers, shaman, whatever they call them. If I was called that, I don't think I want to be around because I'm not an imitator. I don't pretend, I don't imitate nobody. I talk about the *Wakangli*, the electricity and all that and we talked about the battery, the car battery and see it didn't start and it took that one, he hooked it from that energy so that it revived. I can rely on him. He is sitting there. It has to come from one energy to the elder and his wisdom goes to the young, they work together and it works.

Right now, that woman, she's not all here because part of her is at home with her husband. And her husband, he's not all there, part of him is over here worried about her and she worry about him and they're worried about Uncle Sam. I don't have an Uncle Sam, I have an Uncle Bill. He writes to me every month. Pay up now or else you gonna be afoot. I don't worry about Uncle Sam. He worked his way in here, in the Lakota Nation. Now he says you have nothing, this is all mine. He forgot about God, the Creator. He is stingy with me, so be it. He's going to be stingy with you. I'm having a hard time, you said it, I didn't. You're going to have a hard time.

I'm a good nurse, you're a good nurse. Oh, I don't know. I still have to go for masters and doctors and I need a whole bunch of doctor's degrees, PhD's, post-hole diggers degree. I guess that's what they call it, PhD? If they're masters, I like to see the masters of the PhD. They could have bachelors degree. You probably have that. How many husbands or boyfriends do you have? You're probably the only one with bachelors degree. You turn that around. Can't say I have a bachelors degree. I have a masters degree, I have a doctors degree but she don't have none of this, you don't have, I don't have, you have bachelors degree. Those boys, they're single unless they have bachelors degree because they're bachelors. So who made all of this law that you must have these to tell and stand in front of people and tell that you know it all?

One nephew, he was going to a Sundance, going to Martin, try to get there before store closed, you know. He was right, but he had no right to point a finger at me. He made a commitment. He wants an Eagle feather tied on his head during Sundance. Car's, trucks and pick-ups going. He saw me coming, he ran a red light, show off. He went like that, I turned that finger this way. I don't know what it means but that light went out and he just kept on coming. I think my son and one grandson was in there. He just laughed. "What did you do or say Grandpa?" Well, confidentially, I said, when he pointed a finger at me he called me dirt but I turned my finger up and this is not bad. "I said up your ass or you get a spanking." He just had his pampers off here a few days ago I think.

He's going to have nightmares from here on till Sundance cause his job ends June. That other one was in there, he said, "When are these young punks going to learn Grandfather, not to tell you what to do?" He said "One time one of them point a finger at you so you went like that and that car just stopped and went this way, they parked and got out and checked their car and they didn't know what to do." These fingers they can do things like that, but it's for correction. You have to be patient, sit and behave yourself, keep your mouth shut and try to learn something. The good, take it and help someone.

This year it's going to be kind of hard for some of them, but with me and the ones that listen it's going to be easy. Floyd called the other day and said, "Dad, I don't think I can go out there like I used to but is it alright if I take a chair and sit back there cause I was told there was going to be doctoring?" I had a cane, I went out there and while you prayed, I prayed too. And you had your age standing there without a cane smiling using your cane. There I was, I was mocking you. "I didn't know you was mocking me." he said, "I guess I will never get my degree I'll just go on with the future as rookie the rest of my life." He said it, I didn't.

But I said, "Don't forget to put up those toilets, I need eight of them. Think about number nine, we might have to put one up for children. And that means about a foot and a half up and small hole so that six foot person cannot sit there. You have to have somebody get people to clean those outhouses every morning and a garbage truck going every evening and morning."

Dean Martin, all those cowboy shows. You know at the end he always gets killed by the Jim Bowie knife, is that how they say it? He's always has a knife. Sitting here like, I dreamed of those boys, they bought a pair of boots, snake boots. I'm pretty sure he's not, he might be crazy, but he's not stupid enough to wear those out here now.

And there's this old farmer, his name is Russell, his last name, he used to live out there. He had an old truck standing there. Traditional, this is all that's left, he said. The boys were there. He said, "You see this post?" All those posts were in line. One moved but they keep on going. The funny thing, these are all iron posts and they're painted red on the top tip. So tell them as a young man, young person, you walk that, but things change, a few inches, or whatever, but still go straight and you learn so that the next one that comes might try to straighten that out, last time.

And here, this brother-in-law he sitting there with those boots, sitting like this and rubbing his head and laughing away, you know. And his boots are muddy and have green grass. Gee, why ruin a pair of boots like that, you know? And I got to thinking, maybe their plastic. But I didn't talk to him, he was just smiling and laughing. He was happy facing west.

He said, "It's really *Lila oiyokipi* over there." If you want to go I said go. He was talking on the phone. You're all crippled, you can't do nothing, you hate to tell stories, or your life story or something good, you just go ahead and go. He said, "Okay, I'll tell him but right now this oxygen, I'm going to take it off cause I got to go outside and have a cigarette." He died of cancer, then when I went to the funeral his casket was sealed. But It is always still alive, life goes on.

You girls, there's three of you here with me the last couple days and He's already picked you. One day you will do my work, the work I've been doing. Fifty-four years is a long time. Four years before I married, way before that, sixteen years old. Only pleasure I have left is probably that cigarette. I don't even know how to make that so I sit here and you seen me and sometimes I break it and go get you a cigarette and I'm alright. Cause this person's already picked but that don't mean I'm gonna die. I want to enjoy. Didn't know enough and learn enough and know enough to make people happy.

There's a man had a vision about the Circle with no end. There are one hundred nations, one of the stragglers, he's from Greece, he got lost, he got lost here in America. He found a place and that Eagle feather was on the ground. Floyd picked it up and give it to her and he came in and they fixed it and he hung it for hundred and one nations. Now, all over this world how many nations are there? Can somebody tell me? How many languages are there? With that one hundred nations. Julius, he smudged, and three men they sing and they took a woman, a chain of reaction. Now this person is going to see all those languages, through miracle going to understand and no need to worry about jokers, they are already there.

There is no one can say I am a *Heyoka.* The truth is, I never seen anybody walking backwards. There was only one person did and he cried on my chest, times going to be hard for me isn't it, Grandpa? Yep. You're given that gift. You're gonna help young people. You make people happy. You have one ring circus, I said. You see monkeys, all kinds of animals in that Circle of one.

I appreciate this weather, beautiful. He got to see all that beautiful out there. Trees are beautiful. You never see this day again, but He said, "my words will go on." And He said, "at the end of time a lot of these dreams its beautiful." There'll be no Bear Butte, that's where I'll be. The new land, it's beautiful. It'll be hills there and the future more hills. All this, when they talk about this, people will start with where White Buffalo Woman came. Just like a little puppy story. Got so people were hungry, cold whatever. They have no where to go, no way, which ever way to go, to survive. Now everything goes back to the chief. So he prayed and he prayed for wisdom and understanding how to survive with his people. Probably not hour, but days, weeks, months or maybe a year he prayed. He suffered and his people suffered.

One day a couple of warriors went out. Young men went out to scout around to see what they could find, game of some sort. They could make a big kill and go home and feed the people. Here they come to a place, sort of remind me of the Badlands, here they met this young woman. All from nowhere She appeared. And one was sort of wise, I guess, and one was foolish. He didn't know he was foolish till the young girl appeared. The foolish one, all he thought about was how beautiful She was, negative things come to his mind. And the other one says, "Be careful, this, what ever it is, She came from nowhere. It might be *Wakan*. Might be a Holy thing." But the other says no, he said, "I'll find out." He ran, got up to Her and sure enough She said, "Come into my wrapping." and he did.

All there was was smoke, probably smudge like, you know. Not dust, but smoke. And he saw there, his friend laid there, just bones. She said to the other one, "You go back and tell your chief, your people that I will be coming and I will bring you something that you can hold and pray with. It's going to be Holy. And you will survive. But first must pray for understanding and help and walk with thanks every day of your life."

So he went back and She told him what all to put up, what was needed. She told him how to do this and do that, instruct him. So he went back running and told them that he met a woman, a young lady, that She was going to come tomorrow. She's bringing something for us to keep to have so that our people will survive. And next day, I guess the chief stayed up all night, probably most the people and they prayed that nothing bad would come, as it is they were having suffering, here comes that same woman. So he said, "Here She comes."

She had a bundle with her and She placed it in front of the chief and She unraveled it. Here that's the first *Cannunpa*, Calf Pipe. It didn't say *Cannunpa*, it says Calf Pipe, *Pte San Wi*. She told them how to set up the altar, and how to pray. She made a Circle around it, the directions, how to pray and sing and She sang a song about the *Cannunpa*. *Cannunpa Nicaupi*. She was to mend the break in you.

They say whatever this Calf Pipe is, *Nicaupi,* they're bringing you that and it's healed. Through the Spirit of God it was brought, She was like the angels like they talk about in the Bible, I guess. And this is the way you do it before you pray. She put tobacco in and the Spirit of God will be there. And remember don't fool me because this is *Wakan,* it's Holy and when you load It up you sing this song and whatever you want you will receive repeating the song. When you do this *Tunkasila* the Creator, the God, the Great Spirit, will come and see you, and all your prayers will be answered. And the chief, he picked certain ones for his helpers and he always warned them that this is *Wakan,* the *Cannunpa.*

It is brought to the men and the truth has never been told. So even young people that carry the *Cannunpa* now, they don't know why. They imitate their mom and dad. And I don't know the white men came in with the word shaman, imitator, make believe, model someone and the religion that this Lady brought.

She said, "I will come and see you again," and She went so far and threw Herself on the ground and it changed color from white, some said it's a *luta*, it's a red dress She wears, some said a light buckskin, *ptesawe* means gray. So maybe She came in a gray buckskin dress or nobody really knows the material. She went so far and pulled Herself down and rolled over and a different color come up again. She did that again, each time a different color.

And later Christianity come. It came in. Overseas they call it the birth of Christ. But that already happened here on this Turtle Island. South America to Canada, there is a connection there. That's why many people say Black Hills is the center of Earth. But others say, "No, wherever you go it's the center of the earth." But those arguments will go on and on until it's time. So there are songs that go with every ceremony. That lady shows the chief so he can go ahead. The doctoring starts there.

So without the *Cannunpa*, without the Lakota group of people get together, if the Lakota's not there, there is no power there. Now days they call it cult, a devil worshipping and even there if there's no person that the evil's not in it, it's just a cult. A bunch of people is organized, they imitate like any church. The church is all organized, man made rules.

Remember that workshop, all of you girls and women sit in a Circle. Grandma said, "You gonna do a dog." I guess that scared you. Grandma said, "pretend it's a chicken." Your mind was negative. What you teach them, how to butcher that puppy. That's a medicine. The dog has a lot of power to heal. After it was finished Steve was playing around and stuck his whole hand in there, that kettle. Took piece of it, hmmmmmm-mmm, just like that. *Pejuta waste*, huh, good medicine. So he took the drum stick, he called it and started at one end and took a bite and next person took a bite. And some of those people, their necks was that long you know. Then he wiped it all over one of their foreheads. There's power in that puppy.

103

Then she went home and had nightmares for two weeks trying to understand why you would eat a puppy. Took her years to understand. Really it took her a long time to get that one, and she's still getting it. If you can eat fish, you can eat puppy, steak, snake, if you can eat pork, you can eat chicken. This is more pure than all that other stuff. That big hog will eat anything that is thrown to him. There's power there.

Some will miss Bear Butte, I guess. All those people that are use to a big crowd and see who can out pray someone and who can out sweat and out cook. Gee, I don't know what kind of weather we'll have here. We are going to have to prepare ourselves. There will be no hotels, motels. Last year I had the cramps, my leg cramped. Oh, my legs cramped. She rubbed my legs and oh boy, I thought I was going to kick the bucket there. Those two say, we got you a room at Sturgis. I said you take us, huh. Well, we got to there, maybe it's here at Sunny Inn or something. They didn't say which motel. We thought they'd probably be standing out there. They got there. They were already in their room. How do you know, we didn't tell you the room. Well, one of the girls, and the old lady they got to thinking the Sun Inn so we went to Sun Inn and sure enough there they were.

There was no game up on the hills, the rivers are dry, not dry but no fish, not even a cottontail. People are hungry. So there was this little boy, he said, "Maybe I should go up the hill and pray. Maybe the great God will answer me and show me a way. So he went up to pray sitting with his little puppy." No one really said how long, but he fell asleep, I guess, and when he woke there was no puppy and something touched his ear, wet. He looked, here was a horse standing there, color of his puppy. There is someone here, he heard a voice. It said, look beyond down the valley or behind the flats or prairie. It said, there is game, Buffalo. So that little puppy that he names was a *Sunka*. And then that puppy became a horse they called it *Sunka Wakan*.

It's Holy. It's a horse. It's a dog but it's *Wakan*. So he got on his horse and he went back to the camp and he told the people that there were Buffalo. There was no weapon of no kind, maybe a few tomahawks and so forth. And this horse, he was raised by a grandma. This boy gave thanks for seeing all those Buffalo. Now he's wondering how am I gonna do that so my people can eat. He started chasing a few Buffalo and he got ahead of them. And all these Buffalo, he was chasing, chased him.

And there was a big cliff, so he got to that cliff and his horse went one way right or left and those Buffalo kept running, and they went over the cliff. All the women folks and men they went on down and they start butchering. And in Montana or Wyoming there are some cliffs where, I forget what they call it, the Buffalo chase took place.

He went back up and he gave thanks to the great God that his people lived again. So that group of tribe never killed a dog. They don't eat dog unless if it's for medicine and they give it to the *Wakinyan*, the Thunder people, and that becomes that Holy Horse. To make live, *Waniyanpi* they call it. It's a living thing. It's sacred. It can protect you, it can warn you and that again it can bring life and it can kill. If you don't feed it, it will get hungry and it will attack anything, even a little kid.

So whatever animal you are suppose to take care of, whether it's a bird or an ant or whatever. So that's the puppy story. And it says some people going to play with us. Like some people say I love you, and some they don't love you. They don't show it but they bug you to play with you, and some love you and some hate you. Just like they do a little puppy. And still you have to forgive those people.

It's kind of sad to see these boys have these dogs tied up in a cage and not feeding them. Little *Spula*, Grandma's dog, is like a princess. She's spoiled. She wouldn't last five hours outside. Standing there, she'd probably freeze. So many times these dogs we abuse them or we don't feed them or we don't treat them right and yet they wag their tail humbly and still they forgive us. The human being they might forgive but they don't forget. But a dog will forget and forgive. Tomorrow is another day. That's a lesson itself.

Those people, some tribes, they don't eat the dog. Out here, in the *Yuwipi* ceremonies, they use them but I, myself, don't believe in that. If I am going to sacrifice anything it would be myself, give myself to God and try to do better tomorrow, be better tomorrow. I don't know, I may be strange. People say, if you don't believe in it, then why have we done it at Bear Butte? You didn't see me do it. The last couple of years they have brought those puppies back. They call one Bear. One of the boys brought one back. They told him to take care of it. His name was Lucky. And he died in his pickup truck. He had to get rid of the pickup cause he didn't take care of that puppy.

So with me it's the whole thing. One time only. I was told by a medicine man, "Take that puppy up there and face it East." He said, that puppy was all colors, all the rainbow colors like *Tunkasila* to remember all the colors, sage and put it there facing West. I did and look where I'm at today. Between that and myself I have to give myself to *Tunkasila* so that puppy can have a life, go on living.

So many medicine men they call it sacrifice. They believe to put on a ceremony you have to have one of those puppies, but I myself don't believe that. Cause *Wakinyan*, the Thunder People, they are already with us, with the electricity we have, the car battery. *Wakangli* they call it. So we don't have to wait for January or any month now. When you turn that electricity on it's already there. The air, the water, and whatever makes electricity. And when that goes out you don't have no light. You will stop, everything in your home will stop, quit. You got to give it respect. The Thunder Being, is a winged great one, it lives in the west. When you hear thunder, that is it's voice. When the book says, "The word was," maybe it means this first thunder. It's eyes send lighting bolts to bring, join, Heaven and Earth, like bridge. These sacred beings bring us life, the water to live, living water. Then we feel joy, the rain washes us, our cares, then comes the smell after. The Eagle is a part of this. It is the messenger. When you
see that Eagle pray, Grandfather,
Tunkasila, is standing there.

Sit and listen. One of these days some of those *Takoja* grand kids gonna ask you about a story and if you don't know you better come up with something real fast. Think of some. All Grandmas should know at least 10 stories of some sort. Legend or make-believe or make-up something that is benefit. You girls have a Sweatlodge and have Grandma tell you stories. I need some storytellers. It's important to the young people. Listen to Grandma tell a story, you might learn something.

I was in the hospital one time and I was laying down there and a real nice looking young man came. He had dirty overalls on and a homemade shirt and he had a little dirty bag and he put some medicine like this and he said, "your brother has these but, he doesn't want to give them out to you." He showed it to me. Sitting on my bed, there was a lady next to me and here she was singing a ceremony song so I sat up and I looked at her. Here she was sound asleep, that woman. So I stood there. I said to this lady, I said, "Geeeee! You sang some pretty ceremony songs." And here she said, "Mam, I never liked to learn to sing." She said, "I don't know what that is, but my husbands a minister, an Episcopal minister, and that's the only place we go to church." And I said, "Yeah, you did, you sang songs." And here she took her ring off, the only ring she had on, with a little pearl on it and she gave it to me. She said, "That was really good of you to hear me like that." And she gave me that little ring. About two weeks later she passed on, that woman, she's from Wanblee. It really scared me!

Storytelling, there is a good one I heard once. A Cherokee man he dressed in red and white. He said, "We all getting do whatever we want, but we can never, never kill a true God-picked medicine man. You see a lake," he said, "a huge Buffalo be standing there and little Buffalo came up and he swallowed that Buffalo. Another one showed up and he swallowed it. There was a little medicine man who pretended to be real medicine man so this big Buffalo standing there swallowed them."

It's just like pointing a finger at someone, three more are pointing back at you.

Some say, there is a Lakota Medicine Man, they say he is a Medicine Man. People be careful of what you say, your swallowing yourself. It's just like pointing a finger at someone, three more are pointing back at you. That finger comes back to you. This is what he is saying. And he sat next to me and he said, "These people don't understand. They have ministers and doctors and yet the natural doctor they don't understand him. The natural minister they don't understand. He uses his hands to heal, he uses fire and water." I didn't understand what he meant by that. But maybe he saw something there I didn't see.

The word target, he is their target. Every day they throw arrows at him. His back is all scarred, from back biting. They say good things and then they turn right around and say bad things about him. But it is always in the back. He pretends to mind his own business but stay there and prays and later he sees the results. And somebody goes in there and takes all the credit but he doesn't care because at the end of time the truth will be out. Gee, that's a long puppy story, isn't it?

Try and learn. You might have some good stories. I don't know. But there is always little tiny stories usually, they call them parables, isn't it? You have to use something. One time I told Bat to bring a object lesson so he took Colgate toothpaste and a toothbrush and he brushed right in front of the congregation, he brushed his teeth. "Now," he says, "all the sins is out. I washed them. So nothing bad is going to come out of my mouth." "But one thing I forgot," he says, "how do I brush my brains? What shall I use for my heart? We can use soap, wash our clothes with soap but how do we get to our hearts, our minds?" Later, of course, he had heart surgery and so have I. They opened him up a couple of years ago, remember? And we joked about it. But he said, "I think they forgot one more rock in there. They should have gotten all of them out, because if I try to think negative or say there is some wrong thing that little tiny rock is in there so he can teach others right and wrong."

So some of the Sundancers, you know, they don't go through these surgeries for nothing. There's a story in it that somebody may live. But all you hear is *Cannunpa, Hanbleceya, Inikagapi* and we want to watch you Sundance. They think that's all there is. But each and everyone of those Sundancers, their helpers are, the Creator's helpers. Cause they have a chief to listen to and take their instruction from, and get busy and try to save some souls, but some don't. They don't teach anything. The man sits there and he teaches women folk, so women folks, out there, out in the world they go by a man's teaching.

Like saying Lakota, *hiye'*, instead they say *ho*, man's way. And some they want to be drummers they say certain tribe, I belong to that tribe and yet she uses a word *Mitaku Oyasin* and the song she sang probably Four Directions, it's Lakota song, that's all she know. *Iktomi* somehow that spider got hold of that person. She or he is sure nice people, but I wouldn't want to be caught with that person cause it's thin ice that persons walking on. One day it's going to come back to them. So I told out there, if someone comes into the Sweatlodge, use the language that you're brought up with. If you don't know how to sing these Lakota songs, first you must learn the words, the meaning, what it means and when you sing it you sing it right so you get good answers.

112

Women go in without men, or you see that man and not *Tunkasila.* Smudge yourself, means use few *Inyan,* rocks, little bit of water, not 20 rocks or 5 gallons of water. Just women must go in there and take that cover off, at least to the waist. When we open the flaps then you cover up. They sit there with all those clothes and just imagine what are those clothes made of, what kind of fabric, what kind? There must be dyed and have some chemical in it, of some sort. So the teaching goes. Always tell women to learn and teach the right words, teach them the right way to sing. What to use and what not to use. What to say and what not to say.

I heard a women sitting there and one of them started praying Tunkasila, and that women said Ho! She pretend to be Grandfather. Instead of saying, she should have said sister or Grandmother tell Grandfather and Grandfather will tell the Creator. Chain of command, but right there she killed it. This lady said to the Grandfather and she said *Tunkasila* and this women said *Ho*! She became a man, she's a women.

So these are things that need to be taught. Try and pray right. Use the right words. Proper words. Dress properly. If you go in a Sweatlodge all you need is a housecoat now. Maybe a little towel that you wipe your face with. You go in there put that housecoat down and there you are. You're whole body is mush. Instead you go in there with long Johns and bra and belly tightener whatever they call those, girdle, whatever, or dress.

You may as well stand underneath that shower and take a shower, you know. Men likewise. At least they come close cause they have shorts on and a towel and they go in. So work on the women, teach the women. Those housecoats are easy to get. And that's what you use when you go in there they close flaps take it off. When it's time to open put it back on. Some of this material it can burn you, stick to your skin, blister you. Use that pure, that cotton from the Mother.

These ceremonies are Holy, don't play. When you go into the Sweatlodge you go back before your birth. Inside your Mother, you pray, ask for Her help, Her understanding. We give back. We pray. Be careful what you promise in there.

Those four directions, they hear you. Each has a Grandfather sitting there. That *Cannunpa* is there. Some want to jump right in. Spirit tells these things sometimes one, two, many before dream or vision, then that Circle opens. Prepare, tobacco ties, thoughts, service, humble all these things. Pray use that *Cannunpa* then take to that one who represents *Tunkasila*.

Some Lakota women know traditions. They remember respect for their men. These men are protectors of women and children, men they must have respect, it goes both ways. Men eat first, then children, women eat later. None better, or slave, or abuse like some say, just respect. Never forget the elders, give most respect here. The, *Wacisu,* white people are told, "Look me in the eye, then I know you our telling truth." Our way, Lakota way, is to keep eyes down when talking, that's respect.

Remember that Spirit plate, not just for ceremony, every time you eat. Life is ceremony. Take a little bit of everything put it on a nice plate, not one of those paper things, walk out away where no one walk. When you give a plate, use a little bit of all that. Pray as you put it on, use fine plate, you know, honor those. Don't forget the coffee and cigarette. I may get really thirsty over there. Find a good place, maybe where no grass grows, sacred. You feel. The Spirits come and feed, maybe coyote, dog, who knows, all that is sacred. Find the right place, and say a prayer. Remember those ancestors, the Spirits, *Tunkasila*, the Creator. In this way you remember yourself. This is sacred *Wopila*.

Life is ceremony

You and you and you, I need volunteer now. Just the lazy people they can go Sundance. Just the lazy people can go sit on top the hill pretend to pray. *Tunkasila*, Grandfather, bless me and what are you going to do after he blesses you. Come down or what are you going to do? Don't tell me you seen a vision, fell asleep or dream there because I'll see it in your life you know. That's the kind of vision you saw.

And I have a lot of work for woman. Those rose bushes, there going to be bunch of them. What do you call those little blades? Thorns, I need a bunch of those so they can say *Tunkasila* give me the understanding and the courage and the strength. Get a little bag and throw it in there, for Sweatlodge, start saving canvas, tarp, whatever they are going to use so they can go in there. Men folks fix their own. Women folks help get wood a little bit, and a few rocks. After all, their going to use it too. Some of them have already started giving me dirty looks, hmmm, so that's how it's gonna be. Women ain't suppose to do that I guess. Women a long time ago they have blankets, they haul wood, they haul the water.

The men folks go out there Buffalo, Elk whatever. They tell me they used to carry those Deer on their shoulders. Now you take one of these young men, slap a Antelope on their shoulders they go down cause they're that weak. They eat too much pork, too much beef, not enough Buffalo, no strength, no muscle.

That kind of makes you wonder, doesn't it? You ask how come you don't eat Buffalo, when you say the rest of them should eat Buffalo. I eat little Elk meat, little Bear meat, little Deer meat. This year they make you strong and swift and all that. No need to go out there and hunt anymore because I have my angels. They can do all the providing for me you know. So God, He said you will not use angels. He can use angels but I can't. And these people have to be pure. I cannot trust some with the Holy things. They are still down here. They try to grab something that they figure that will give them life.

And we know where Jesus came from. The Lakota people came from overseas to this land. They said we didn't know God, from overseas to here and they call us atheists or savages or whatever. Now look at now, now days, what they brought and where is the Indian at? He was confused. The foreigners forgot to practice what they preach. All for themselves. But now, like I said, *Mitaku Oyasin* and *Wiohpeyota,* and four directions song and *Tunkasila.* Even ministers they go in, Catholic priests and all kinds went to Sweatlodge when their teachings fail.

Every little community has thirty or forty gangs of kids. They say don't touch that kid, that's child abuse. So they make laws so we can't teach our young ones. Now they say the elderly are abused. Now the young ones cannot go to an elder and ask questions. Drug and alcohol they say. Look at the food we eat now. How much alcohol is in that? Cause, they got these cows and they feed them all that corn, wheat and mix and there's alcohol in it. The vegetable you eat there's chemicals in it. And a tablecloth came from heaven, from the sky, landed and Peter said, everything that's on that table-cloth is for you to eat. What goes in that mouth comes out. It don't stay in you. So pray and give thanks as you eat that food. The person that prepares the food, get up at daybreak and pray so that food they handle is gonna do you good. Unless this is done people will be drunks and busybody. That's what you eat, that's what will make you sick.

I don't have much here. All I have is this log house and Sweatlodge and a few trees. This is not even mine. I have nothing here. People can come here and do as they please, but in their ministers home you can't. They will meet you at the door or the church door and if you're well known he might invite you in for a cup of coffee, but you see me, everyone welcome here. Some are good listeners that you can talk to, like that waitress yesterday. So you yourselves have seen these few days. That's me at the beginning and still is and always will be.

118

I don't know that person. We joke about it. You might think I know these people. But I don't. It is the first time I met some of these people. It's just the idea, brain picking. Give a few dollars and you can pick his brain. Give a few dollars and he'll give 'em a story. Before they love me they will have to love *Tunkasila,* they'll have to love almighty God and give themselves to Him like I did. That's all I have just my body but I am a human being. I have temptation in my head. With this craving you people are sitting there nude. You have nothing to hide. I think I have better things I can talk about. I have better things, the trees, the air, the earth, the water. These are four important things in life. So I was scared this last few days. A pretty woman can set up a man. Any prosecutor or judge will believe that lie. That's why the boys they all took off. Then they think if Grandpa trust these people, three women, I guess I'm okay. Do you understand what I am trying to say?

Time will tell, but don't tell me about hard times or I have a problem. I have a problem I have a hard time. I am suffering. Try to get a new land for black and white and set up an arbor where people can think and give us Lakota a chance to talk to Him and get himself ready and then eight, nine o'clock come sit on the ground.

When you were born you didn't come out with a chair. Bring a chair for that elderly and place her. Look, maybe there is a grandma and grandpa sittin' there. Bring a cup of soup. It doesn't matter Lakota, *Wasicu*, whoever it is, Japanese, black people, white people, whoever if they're elderly give to them. Think. Here some soup. They gonna say thank you, *Pilamayaye*. Cup of coffee, hey, look what these people are doing. In the evening, set up something and bring these people together. You been out there. Somebody say here it is. Never mind him, never mind Jim Dubray, he's just stupid, dumb and crazy so he is sittin' out there trying to fast with the rest of 'em. Be friendly. Don't make the rest of the people suspicious that you're trying to do something. Stand back of that elder person. Don't show off in front of them. I can do this, I'm this, I'm that. Don't get in front of no man. Don't get in front of somebody that's praying. He may be praying around the clock. Some have dreams and when it comes to chow time feed that man first and feed that woman unless feed the children first. That's the future. Never mind me, I'll eat last. I don't have very far to go to be on this earth anyway.

I'm no good. I'm the one that mess up everything. Maybe this young one will straighten out these things. Listen and obey. No fireplace, that means no fireplace and if he says fireplace do it right don't dig that hole. You're only digging your grave. That's what all this was about last year, last ceremony. There is a pit there, there is an altar there, there's rocks, a fire and there I was standing there.

I had to call my niece up, and she listened, and she listened to her husband and she listened, and she came but she wouldn't come into the fire with me. There are a few people in there. One man he walked into fire with me. I called him chief that night. He gave Him whatever it is in his hand, he hand it to Him. Next day he said, I want to thank you for giving me that money and he was shocked, you know. You do it in the open.

Time to eat, the fireman. So I said three of you boys move over here, the breakfast starts there. One young man moved when they didn't tell him to move. They said get back there. You don't need to move. That's the first time I saw a white man run in a tipi. He ran, little bitty thing, cause he was hungry. He didn't want to be left out of that Spiritual food. And there was one white woman sat there all through the night. First daybreak I said, hand her that fan. She setting there praying. Her husband still playing around, he's not sure. He couldn't believe this. What's going on?

121

One young man he had moccasins, choker, and a leather fringed jacket. How can this be? You said *Tunkasila*, traditional and then this man he mentioned Jesus Christ, *Wanikiya*. He say I am confused, so whoever his teacher never taught about *Tunkasila*, God, who He is or what He is. I said be patient, if you hang around you might learn something. So right after that this guy break from the gathering and he went to Black Hills and he Sundanced over there. I know some people took off. Their mind is split, they listen, they like to hear me talk but when it's over that's gone. They go where it's easy. But that don't work. They have more power in the main Circle. They compete but they fall on the wayside. They want to stand and prance around, play. So they did. I have eyes and ears in every organization all over the world. Whoever takes off and does something over there I already know. Just before they think or start thinking about it, I know. That's a waste of time.

The community where you live needs help, your family needs help, you need help. It starts right there. Somebody has to listen. This is what I mean. Is it just me, or is it my whole family? I come in a package and that package is gonna go on and it's gonna get more. You don't have to give an account to anybody but *Tunkasila*. Nobody can make you do this and that. Just the Spirit. It's time to do this. Don't have to ask questions. When it comes you move. You do your work. And that's the main thing the Circle has, whatever you do it's a family together.

Try to know every time, everything I go through. People make fun of me watching TV, wrestling, boxing, why how dare you watch those. That's my business. It's my business what I do. If I smoke in here, that's my business. I don't make man made laws. On the front door it says wipe your feet. My daughter made a mistake. I say, give me a wash rag and wash towel. She says why? The sign says take off your shoes and wipe your feet. So I have to wipe my feet. It has no smoking. How can this be. Who am I to make laws. What is good for me is good for everybody, what's bad for me is bad for everybody.

I learned to be patient. I learned that in the hospital. Like always say last person will come first and first will come last. Right now everybody knows everything. You do this, this is good, this is bad. They make themselves into a God. I can't make you do things. But I'd sure like an orange soda now. But the Spirit can make you do things.

There is a lot of reasons to be out there in that Circle. All kinds of talk, like a big family. One time, there was a man, a wife and kids but the wife got jealous and the family break up, she took off. I was told that the kids were crying, the man had prayed and it didn't work. Finally, he went to a hill with a tree and he prayed and he pierced himself to the tree. An Eagle came to the tree and sat on top and the Eagle was singing and he was dancing toward the sun and his wife was going here and there looking for a family which she left behind. That day his prayers were answered, I guess, for she came back and stood there and saw her kids sitting there, her man standing there praying for her and she sang a song. I love that man, I think the world of him.

And here comes that educated lady. She knows it all. White, Indian, it doesn't matter. Black, yellow she crawled into her brains and woke up to fix those bypasses and I happened to come along with a little spark of fire. Not much you know, I'm not educated, just a dumb Lakota and dumb English man a little bit of that. And she happened to spread the word, over here, over there. And that was it for me you know.

A few years or a year later, here she come. A blond. A platinum, bleached, blond. I stood there and she brought a big tall guy and she claimed him, this is my man, what a man. He's Italian. A big huge Italian, mama mia. I know he makes good bread. Makes bread every morning. He has the *Wakinyan* do the baking. I am lazy, but that friend of mine is lazier than I am, so the *Wakinyan* help, he puts the dough in the little machine and in the morning there is, fresh bread. And when we go to the grocery store there is no bread like his. Homemade bread. I don't eat much bread. In the evening I like to eat bread, not with my meal but before I go to bed. Maybe you notice that. I break bread before I go to bed. Maybe a glass of water, juice, cup of coffee, milk.

I try to speak English. Not "melk" but like English-man says milk. Somebody down the line try to make me speak American English they make up words. Got you, gotcha. A lot, to me a lot is a piece of ground, that's lot. The Lakota words today, most of it is all made up. So what happened to it? The white man lost his language. The Lakota lost his language. They lost the culture; I am standing in the middle. The Japanese lost it. The Chicano's, Mexicans, Indians hang by their heel swing-ing. I can go on and on about how they have to learn their way back, how to become Human again and put the Creator, God Almighty, *Tunkasila* first. Sit down and listen to Him patiently. Maybe He was talking to the people before the white man came, they already knew there.

Then a bunch of fire ants come from the East. There was an iron snake that come and an iron Eagle. Those fine red ants were the people of foreign coun-tries. These people, they destroy everything in their path. Here comes the iron snake, that's the train. They even built some snakes to crawl underneath the ground, the subway, I guess. And here comes the iron Eagle. It brought destruction. Later on they call them bombers. They dropped bombs and they kill thousands, millions of people. This Indian still standing at the top of the hill wondering why are they killing one another. The more land they have the more they want, more ground.

125

There's a time coming when, *Tunkasila*, God's going to say enough is enough. Now they dug into the ground, earth, they found a piece of yellow iron they call it gold. The Lakota people they use to have a medicine bundle, *Watawe,* they call it medicine, necklace like. Silver, and ivory and all that. What this Indian is saying to the generation to come, be careful, these people have brought four things.

The *Wowapi Wakan*, the Holy Bible and the second one is, be careful, *Mawakan*, but before that it's *Mni Wakan*, the firewater, the Holy Water they call it. You drink or you go crazy and then the *Maza Wakan*, the iron that pops and kills people and then finally the, *I Wakan* the Holy mouth. It is the heart and mind, but the mouth these four be careful. They can bring many things good and bad but take the good. They are going to hand you a weapon that is more powerful than the ones you have and the ones they have. They are going to point this *Maza Wakan* at you and kill some of you which is delightful.

There's a time coming when, *Tunkasila*, God's going to say enough is enough.

They are going to take all your weapons, bow and arrows, tomahawks and what all goes with it and they are going to hand you a pencil to read and write. They themselves already know how to read and write.

They're going to hand you a machine that goes click, click which is faster than anything, which is typing machine, stronger than a machine gun. Now you take this weapon and you use it well and teach them how to become human. They trying to go around the universe to check out the stars. Now they have flying machines flying around the earth. They even take lightning bugs to put in these satellites. Scientists say there is no God, they're God, themselves. We were warned before many, many years ago. The white people, this man they call Jesus Christ, He was here before. To them this is the promised land, but it is not the promised land. We have to go to the Spirit world, then the promised land, that's where we will be screened. The good and the bad, that's the second sleep.

Death means sleep. To other people when they say dead, died they think that's all over. There is a second death that's coming and that's when we will cry individually for ourselves, our regrets. So this is the way of the Lakota people for many years. My great grandfather say take my children among the Oglala's that they can become Lakota cause this other way, my way, is no good.

We Lakota are fighting among ourselves, to see who's the smartest, and all that politician talk. We never had government like Republican and Democrat we always been independent. We listen to the good, take the good, listen to the bad and if it's bad we let it go.

Yet our councilmen, some of them, fell right in it. No offense, the biggest liars that came out is the one that's holding the high offices. I know that if this word gets out they will send someone after me. Shut him up. He's spreadin' rumors. He gettin' too powerful. That Lakota is gettin' powerful, but he was here first. He's gonna get more powerful toward the Spirit World. So the other people that came from all over the world they made heaven here in America. All the buildings, skyscrapers, clear up a mile high. That's their heaven. Some of them make hell for themselves, with drugs, alcohol, politicians.

All those things have been said. I stand with Mother Earth and the Creator and He gave me one earth, now she became Grandmother. Someone has to be role model. Finally, some of my boys are starting to open up. They start speaking. Today is good day. Some of my sons have died and they resurrect. It's a new life that is coming. The future, maybe, they will work with all nations and try and teach them to become human like God, Almighty, Creator, *Tunkasila* meant to be. So we are concerned for one another. We try to be savior for one another, love for one another, help one another and never sound your own horn.

Our mind is ahead, our heart is not all there. If I teach Lakota culture and language I'll probably throw all the books up in the air. Adios, amigos. I know what would work for you. About 60 rocks and me and you sittin' in there pouring, with a tobacco tie wrapped around your neck. I bet you'd speak fluently. That's what my son was saying. That's the only thing I understand in there is *unsimala ye, Tunkasila, unsimala ya,* have pity on me. Then the old man he said, don't let nobody out when they say *Mitaku Oyasin, they* don't mean it. When they come out it's gone, but if they say *Ina,* it means mama, mother then you open it. Remember, not a sad word for mama and her Spirit will be there whether she living or asleep. So all that lesson last six months, that will be $30 please, thank you. That's fun isn't it. Just tell them we had a good time.

One time an elder, an old man placed me on this, Badlands, and says to me if I ever have go on *Hanbleceya* be careful, *Wakansica,* it's no good, might be a lot of evil Spirits. Many people try to set it up. They call that sheep mountain. But I doubt there is any sheep there anymore. About the last hundred years they call it Kearny Table. People by the name of Kearny, they used to live out there. It's about 200 hundred feet up there. You can see cattle and so forth. Once in a great while you can see deer. But that's very once in a while. But you can't grow a garden, you don't see no trees. You see Cedar trees here and there. I'm glad of that. People from other countries come here and say how beautiful. Maybe if it's beautiful you could call it Goodlands instead of Badlands. In this area you don't see no buildings. The ground is clay, it's hard. So I listen to it.

In 1970's, maybe '75 or '74, '74 I believe, Sundance time, there was a young man got pierced and he was bleeding and he looked down and he talked. I couldn't see who he was talking to but he told about gift. Go get that medicine and he waited about two or three minutes. He said, "He's really slow getting there." About five minutes he looked down and said, "What took you so long? You're good but you're always slow, take your time." He hand me a root. Chop this into little pieces. I had no grinder, no modern grinder to use. He said put it over the wound. Meantime, when this medicine gets on him he is gonna have a dream, he gonna fall asleep, so I did. One of the brothers came up and I told him to put it on him and he did and he quit bleeding. I find out later that he is a bleeder. So his body is full of veins, small, tiny veins. So he had to be careful after that and then he said he didn't need to do that every year. Take care of that body, that's the only thing you gonna have. Why scar it up? It won't be worth anything if you keep that up. Some listen and some don't.

The Sundance song, the singer, brings that song. Like Sundance time, first day we come out, he sings that song, *Tunkasila.* In the Sundance, keep your mind clear, as he sings, he brings these songs up; he chants four verses, four times. These songs are my entrance songs to the Sundance Circle. Every one has a meaning to it. It's my life. When I first started, two, three years ago I came out of the Hospital to that Sundance and I heard all through Lakota country that Sundance song. *Tunkasila* is going to take some of the young bodies and talk to the older ones, elders. He's gonna test them. He's gonna try them. Like the song says, there's future, nothing's impossible.

The rest of them, they gonna have to learn to pray. Size up one another and be happy together again. The girls love their brothers even though they make mistakes. When that sun goes down tomorrow morning everything is new. Never speak a wrong word about your own kids. *Tunkasilia* watches your kids. They come from you, you're only hurtin yourself. Be like a man, they say, love your woman, the one you live with. If you don't love her and take care of her how can you take care of or love your sisters, your mother or your grandmother, likewise, the woman, the man.

Little things I don't forget, they said memory like an elephant. Whatever has been, *Tunkasila* remembers every word since the beginning of your Circle, your life, the day you came out of the tipi, your mother's womb. So what kind of Circle have you got? Is it one of those zig, zag kinds? Or is it straight Circle? There is no end? So after it's finished you start all over again and your children they follow you, they don't listen, they'll come here and there. That Circle kind of bends here and there and then your grandchildren come in but they can't get out. There is no way out. Then your great grandchildren, it's about time you come to that place where there's an opening, not out, but inside it'll open up and go into that so-called Spirit world. It's in there. I don't know if people ever understand what I'm talking about.

Many times I tell my boys read the Holy Bible. Everything that Lakota does, it's all recorded in there. Brother Bat, he found many of them in there. He found one. He got excited. From Rapid City he came clear to Allen, he brought the chapter, the verse. Brother, open your bible. See if it's in there. Same thing. Ezekiel, I'm not saying what chapter or verse. It says like a man walking with his pipe, going up the hill to pray, pray for healing for his people. But before that understanding and by the time he gets back down to ground level some of His friends will have understanding and some will go on same way.

Then in the book of Matthew, read it carefully, it says, one of the disciples says, I will go get tobacco and before you go we will smoke. He said no, when I come back for you people I'll get the tobacco and we will smoke together. It's plain as A, B, C. It's right there. They don't flow over, word by word. Because He was here before He went any place else to help people.

It makes you wonder how come two people could start this whole thing. Who was Abel's first wife? Not Adam. Cain? Because there's no other women but just his sister was there. From there, sisters to cousins, second cousin, third cousin, fourth cousin finally the colors they start changing. Some He placed close to the south, the equator, or whatever, closer to the sun. Some are pale, some they look sickly, some Orientals, the Chinese, Japanese, and Philippine's. And the Red people here, they have winter, fall, spring, summer, four seasons. You don't see that in California, Florida, back East. All there is, is snow and rain and summer. What happened to fall and spring? Washington, up north, all there is, is snow and green. They have very short days.

These are some of the things that Lakota say thank you for having such a long day, long night. The sun is still up there and there is so much. Just a word of prayer, yet, to make sure that the nonbelievers have ears you have to walk with them. So you go back and take them and go with them, go with the two, hurt no ones feelings.

But this, at least, is already gone but in the eyes and the feelings of the people that are still there. And someone is gonna suffer a little bit for the people and someone's gonna learn something from this. I felt bad you know, for a little bit there. Why do these young ones have to go through all this? Some are running loose out there and don't care. And His name is mentioned every day, maybe thirty, forty times or maybe three, four dozen time something goes wrong the name is mentioned again.

All in all, maybe we learned something today, maybe later on it will come. But these songs are my entrance songs to the Sundance Circle. Nothing is mine here on this planet earth. Just this body that has been given to me, that's the only thing I have, my skin, my heart, my mind, my tongue, my ears, my nose. This car doesn't belong to me. It's a company car. That's confidential, you know.

Then she came last Sundance. She said, "I have brought you power." Some of you heard that woman talk. Can she teach me, that Sweatlodge? Can she teach me to run the Sundance? Does she know these things? Then she had this little short mini-dress with fringes on it, and everybody just didn't believe or didn't care cause no one said anything about it you know, that's the funny part. The Lakota kept to themselves. If this is ever gonna come back and show itself it be as a young one. Maybe there will be power, then again, the evil maybe coming in place of it.

Maybe the timing is right. Everybody needs to hear themselves. Everybody needs to do that, you need to, I need to. We have to sacrifice something. We have to give up something cause we are afraid. When you look at power or popularity, it'll be gone, but when that happens, there's need in the community, they need help, right there, it begins at home. This is what's happening here. We try to do it together, the old lady, maybe a few of the kids. But some of them, they don't have that trust. That's the way in any culture, any nationality, like you gonna stop America.

There's a medicine man, which they call themselves. Does he trust or is he teaching them? Maybe he's just throwing the pot in there and other people take it and praise him. Hey! He's the holy man. There's nobody holy, only almighty God. *Tunkasila* is the Holy One. He's the Spiritual leader and He's the medicine man and we're just instruments. Remind the patient or whoever it is that tells you about their problems, mistakes, sins or whatever, whose boss.

The so-called leader, I think, needs to be told, like about the tipi. And how can he tell these students that they're gonna have a tipi putting up contest. What they are doing is, they are playing with their momma, grandmother, and their children. These are the know how to people, they call themselves. They turn it into a practice contest. When that day comes, hopefully, none of those *Takoja's* are there when they start contests who can put up a tipi faster than the next school or whatever.

Man has no business putting up that tipi, it's supposed to be a woman. There used to be only four poles, now they use thirty, forty, fifty, or twenty, whatever. They claim that those tipi poles are the children and the cover is the mother and what holds together on top that rope that's the daddy and the little stakes that hold it down from the flaps going up those are the grandchildren that hold them and that's a home, a family. But when that rope gives out, it will fall apart, that home is no more. It's divided. When the cover falls, mother is not there, it is just a shell; the home would be a shell. Dad is up there holding it together, children is there. Next comes the oldest daughter who will carry on the tradition. The top will come loose and the next one goes up there that's qualified. She can hold the family together. When one of those stakes goes, one of the other grandchildren comes and replaces that.

But now look at these buildings we live in, who is holding who? What is holding it together? They say that woman is the boss. The *Wasicu*, white people, call it woman's lib. Women are the boss. They tell their husband when to move when not to move. What to say, what not to say and that's where this Lakota got confused. So these are the things we need to get it together.

Grandma is the boss in this house right now since we don't have the tipi in place of this house. If she has to go before I go this is not a home. There is no cover, no one to pray for us. I'll pray for the children. If I go it's gonna fall apart. My mother and daddy's home when they took off, when they went to the other world look what happened. Now all my brothers are just about gone, one sister is very small but many, many grandchildren. One of my sisters has about sixty, seventy grandchildren but she live in a little motel room with about thirty six of them. If all those get together they can build a home out here, Lakota land. And they don't have to live on welfare. With that many they can help grandma. These are things some of the boys are concerned about.

It's all there, inside.

When I leave these friends of mine, will they go on working with us or are they gonna go and look for something else in other country or look for other medicine man? Then they go and sit and try to take in all they can. Are they going to go on loving my mother? Are they going to drop her right there and go on looking for another grandmother or are they just going to keep on going with us all the way to the end of Circle of life that you take people in? Some help, there're some that don't. They say we know because we spend this much in that family. I wonder if that's enough for that pipe. They think they are trying to buy power or learn something. Those are no, no's.

Lakota people way of life, they don't do those things. They concerned about one another. When one is sick, everybody is concerned. Word gets out there like lightning. What's gonna happen? Like this morning, I said, we'll have to go with the believers and nonbelievers. So we try to bring this white man and this Lakota together and who is the white man and who is this Lakota, this red man? What about these other two directions?

Last night this is what happened. We had the four directions there. And that red man had to doctor the patient. It was weird. They would never understand, even our own people. Those are things that we have got to watch cause we can't let it out. When it comes to heart surgery, there are just certain doctors that are in there. They don't have the whole world in there looking over their shoulder and sticking their nose in there when they don't know nothing about it, they'll mess up the whole thing. They lose that patient. The simple common sense is stay out of that surgery when those doctors start cutting people and taking that out and this and that. What happened is a Spiritual thing, not physical.

My sons and so forth, they talk about it. They learn something from this. Some blame themselves instead doing it here in the family, they went out. And that son is not going to give no answer. They ask him about things but he's gonna keep it. In time he will come out cause he knows more than I do right now and in that Circle, that chair, I will be taking it easy. He is the one that's gonna have to answer or give an answer to questions. These visions, dreams, they start coming. Man's life is changing. That's the best thing from what happened now.

Everybody, their mind, is at old man Dubray. What they don't know is the main place. Spiritually they think the answer is here and every morning somebody comes here, noon and evening, people come and visit. They think they have nothing. It's all there, inside. But here, the Sweatlodge, everything is here, so while I'm here it's gonna be here but after I'm gone it's gonna move back and so that's where it going.

Those who are gonna come in and stay awhile and move they better get all they can. Some have workshop every weekend instead of using their own culture they use the Lakota, *Cannunpa, Mitaku Oyasin*, they sing the Four Directions song, Lakota. So these ones are getting their prayers answered?

I can pray in any church, Catholic, Episcopal, just name it. I probably can preach like Oral Roberts, Billy Graham and produce money. Money is their tabernacle. Huge colleges they put up, they use that. They are creating Christians they say. But are they? Only God can do that. *Tunkasila* is the only one He can touch heart and make those things happen. People can go on searching. They say they going to keep searching, searching, look, and look but they gonna die. They never gonna find, maybe, because, I'm already with them. He is in me and I in them. It's trinity like, you know?

And there are four angels I will not use. What does He mean by that? So He picked man and woman and advertised His coming. Lakota way, He's coming and He taught us how to pray. And we know where He came from and still Lakota called savages. People came from overseas to here and told us we didn't know God and they call us atheists or savages or whatever. Now look at now, now days, what they brought. Where is the Indian? He was confused. The foreigners forgot to practice what they preach, all for themselves.

But now, like I said, *Mitaku Oyasin* and *Wiohpeyota* and four directions song and *Tunkasila*. Even ministers they go in there, catholic priests and all kinds went to Sweatlodge.

There is Prairie Dog Town they call. That's where the old lady got her medicine. It helps people that believe. If you listen and do likewise nothing is impossible. But she had to pay for it with her body. So I thought I'd throw that in there. That's one place you might stop and say, thank you, *Pelamayaye*. But you gotta make sure if it's a right Spirit or an evil Spirit. It's her story to tell.

I was watching Waylan when he was a baby. I put him in a stroller and I was scared of that couch. I was home with him most of the morning and here I was sitting there and cutting up pieces.. And you know all of a sudden I was gone. I was sitting there and I was gone. Here I was going through a fence, I didn't even stoop over, go over it, or nothing. I went through that fence and this old man was following me. I looked like this, in here; I had a purple cloth wrapped in something and I said, "Where's my baby and what am I doing?" I was thinking. He went over two pastures and a hill and kind of a Buffalo grass and we went up through there. He said, " Aha, Takoja, what you got there?" He said, "Spill it all around , all over."

I took it apart and here is a pipe. I don't know what it was but it had something in it, so I spill it all over the round Circle. "Pick these up, when you get through spilling all this," he said. "Pick these up." and he showed me, ya know. Prairie dog's, you know things that really smell good. "Hold it, put it straight," he said, "put that cloth and put 'em straight in line", he said, and so I did. I picked them up and I shook 'em up and I put 'em good. And load it up, he said, "Now, turn around and sing that song." He sang a song for us. It was you know, the song was very Wakan. He said, "Go home and make it, wash 'em out and boil it this way and give it to that lady." I don't know who this lady was. So anyway we came back and I came back through the house.

It was a wide, pink, square house. It had a porch on there. I went in there and here there was a lady lying on a real old couch with a dirty sheet on. I looked at her but I didn't know who she was. She was just pitiful. So I went in there and I start boiling water and I put that medicine in it. You could just hear a rattlesnake and those little prairie dogs. You could hear them in that boiling water. And he said, "Come and give it to her when it's green, like so." I had some great big cups, long time ago. So I took one to her. I made it cold, ya know, and gave it to her. I had it in my hand and I prayed and I turned around this way and that way. When I turned on the last turn I hit the door and when I hit the door it woke me up and I didn't have nothing in my hand.

Nobody was home at my house and so it just scared me so bad, you know. I just sat there and I wondered what was happening to me. I didn't even cook dinner for the workers. You know it scared me. So I picked up my son and changed his diaper and gave him a bottle and it was noon hour when I came to myself. It bothered me so badly, you know, it just makes me want to cry. Why did this happen to me? So when he came back I told Grandpa about it, what happened to me and here that afternoon my brother came, for no reason he came. He said, "What's wrong?" I don't know how he knew. I told him what happened to me and he said, "Well, I'm gonna have a ceremony. I'm gonna ask what it's for." And after that, things happened and he was waiting for the answer. He kept waiting and waiting and he never did find out what happened. He said, "Somebody close to you is going to bring you some medicine." And here out of the sky-blue one of my brothers was working near here, he put that medicine in a big paper sack and brought it to me. It was really funny. Up to this day I always wondered. It was medicine, and he told me to give it to that woman.

Where that medicine come from, where did he pick this up? He said, I'm gonna tell you. Later in the years around Scenic he said on this side of Scenic, *Iyuksan,* means the turn, *Ipa,* means little butte. He said, this is where that pejuta is at *I-pa-ekta,* the medicine is at the top, right here. This is where the medicine is at. But you have to be authorized to find it.

143

The individual they're gonna stand overnight there around the corner facing East coast. Their gonna see a whole lot of things. On my left I picked up a root but that wasn't it. It was there coming back from the North. It was on my left side, left, yeah, left. Just like my dad said, you find a corner stone you'll find treasure. First thing come to my mind when he said that, before he passed on, after that I always looked for a corner stone. If I can find that stone, maybe he hid a coffee can full of money, but that wasn't what he was talking about. Later in the years, I found the corner stone and I lift that stone, beneath that was the treasure of life. Everyday I thanked him for it. That's why I told one girl never talk about your mom, how cruel she was to you, instead of saying bad things about her, telling negative things about her, say thank you, pray for her, she brought you into this world and that might be enough. She's in the Spirit world or half way there or whatever.

On my mother's side were very important people just like Crazy Horse was back then. We never talk about it. I don't know where they put this and that in this world you know to go back all the way to the family tree. My Dad's mother she's a Kills An Enemy, and my Dad carried that name when he came back from the First World War. They go by what the people see in them; they name them after an activity or whatever. Buffalo, Deer, Circle around the Tall and whatever. She's related to Sittin'Bull. We never talk about it.

I remember my mother said, one medicine man she met at the Sundance, that's where *yuwipi* come in. He's the only one that I know. There might be some before him. But the ceremony to me it's kind of scary. One of my brothers and I, we went first time, we were gonna take it easy but, that elder said, "*Takoja*, grandson, he want to sit still." *Wakinyan* will take care of you and make sure that you sit still. There was a skeleton in front of us, lightning, it sounds like, the Eagle come and slapped us around a little bit.

The ceremony started when the sun went down. All those people he give them channels to pray and he interpret their visions, dreams, whatever. He did a lot of healing. That's where old man Fools Crow got his, he told me and from there, a few people inherit the power. They don't just have it. You have to prove yourself that you're worthy. Then one day Fools Crow was sitting there and he says, "This belonged to Crazy Horse and it's suppose to come back to you, the family." She took it; prayed with it, cried with it and out of there he gave me two center feathers and now I carry that. When it comes out, that one I have now, every year they dance under that.

All those *Cannunpa* there they mean nothing to me. When I'm gone they can proudly replace it with one, but the people, that's the main thing, smoke the *Cannunpa*.

The one that's the Spiritual one. I think I know where it's at. The *Wasicu,* white man, came up with a design what they call catlanite. He came up with that design. That's where that came from. Now they have Buffalo, birds and what all goes with it. Whatever turns them on.

So my cousin, sister could bring me something like that. Like long time ago they give each other maybe *hamikceka,* moccasins with, *takan,* is a sinew and *hanpsicu,* like Buffalo? So I got little pieces in the garage now. They've used the rest of it. They give me that from the tribe. I forgot Grandma used everything. Brains, they wash it, they put flour on or salt. Those are all good. They used to eat part of everything I know too. They boil it and boil it and went to town. It's *tah,* what do you call it, *taniga?* The Inside of a Buffalo? Gonna take about six hours boiling.

My mother-in-law said, "I'm cooking there, get me some of those, some chips." In Lakota talk she said, when you come by that kindling, the wood, throw it in the stove, cooking stove, put chips in there. Every one of them come in and put those chips in the soup jug. We all got scolded! She made us spill that, and wash it and put it over again and use hominy. Gee, it was really big. Remember the pigs feet? You could hand her anything and they'd eat it.

Everybody is involved with this cause that snake is not going to let you go. The thing is you got to think positive cause that's part of the Creation. I'm being protected here. If there's something wrong it makes it right. Running it makes you sick, if somebody's running it, why not stop? One has stopped, one is running. They're brothers, they are all right. Time someone has to stop. The big one, he'll get there sooner or later. Later is better than sooner I guess. Have to have patience there.

All this, must have started way, way many years ago. Let's put it that way. All a sudden, that beautiful woman, you know, instruct him, do this, this way. White Buffalo Woman brought understanding, wisdom to that one person. She instructed him how to make where he was settin' gray, but he didn't have the altar. He must have an altar, so she taught him what to use for that altar. Only she could go in front of it cause she has the power. Other people after that show respect. And he went along. As She left, that Buffalo it turned into different colors. When she got to the hilltop he saw this one color. She came with this one color but in between there were four colors, at the hilltop just one color.

He went out and took young men and taught younger people how to pray. After that, every ceremony or whatever it is you call it, a song goes with it. So he prayed and told people he prayed first and then he sang a song and he put that in words and he smudged himself and He didn't know how to get hold of the Spirit, communicate with the Spirits that She told then that's where Vision Quest comes in.

Then years later Sundance come into the picture, not only here in United States but this happened in Europe. I forget Egypt, India or someplace, I think Egypt and then Pharaoh stopped and talked to King David, he stopped him cause people started playing with that like what they are doing now you know. "No more Sundance," he said. "No more cutting the flesh." About time you put it away. We all make mistakes, you made it too.

And years later He appeared back here in the United States, so called. He came in, in Spirit. The other side, later in the year, like Moses and so forth, Bible time, Moses, Christ came along and then it was told that He was here first. First the lake, river, or whatever, a bunch of kids and women are cleaning up or taking a shower or not shower but swimming. The same man appear and He stayed with them a while. One day He said He was going other place and talk to some people. He called it the salty water. Where is this salty water? Have

you ever tried to drink ocean water? I guess it is salty.
Many years later Christ came back all scarred up.

Those people had no respect. Respect is gone and
that is relationship of Mother Earth. Don't take this personal I myself I call it a retreat. Right now I'm retreat-
ing here. Maybe a day or two or three I'm ready again.
How far I came for this retreat. I'm not alcoholic, I'm
not on drugs. A person needs to retreat back up a little
bit to an ice age. Only way they can get hold of you is to
ask Spirit. This summer time you know what I'll have is
a sleeping bag and below here that's really retreat. Get
away from all this.

Many of us haven't learned anything from the Eagle yet,

You pick a female and a male Eagle which one
lays with egg? The female. She moves and who sets
on it? The male. The female travels all over and the
male he protects that nest. One or two little eggs and
they fly around and the teaching goes on. Many of us
haven't learned anything from the Eagle yet, I don't
think. When I first came out here I was telling there's an
Eagles nest. I call it Eagles Nest. Somebody takes care
of this place they call *Tokala* warrior. This place really
has to be watched cause if it's left open you don't know
what's coming in good and bad. This is where there's
women always there, flying, protecting the male.

Some years ago I met a woman I think she had long hair way down, black, like black choke cherries, um, um! Boy my eyes crossed-eyed. I couldn't talk, I felt like crying and years later one morning I got up, I looked and she was gone. As I looked at the table a pair of glasses was there, a pair of dentures was there. I said, "What happened?" A young woman used to lay along side of me. This morning there is an old lady, a Grandma. Whew! For a second I thought I had the wrong woman. But I still see her as that young woman. I still have a confession to make to Catholic priest. That was a terrible thing I said.

Coming down the road, that man was no master, but he said, "Mister Dubray? Your woman over there?" "Yeah, she's one of them," I said. He looked at me. "I heard about that. A chief has many wives, medicine man has many wives. How many?" he asked. Joking, I said, "Sixteen. And your sister-in-law, eight years old, she's coming in." She called me father. He got all mixed up.

For love or for the truth so Jesus came back. But He said one day I will be back. And He stood on top of hill and showed them how to pray, taught them how to pray. And the lady shows up in his place and taught the Lakota people how to pray in front of the altar.

Straighten out that medicine wheel, the wagon wheel, like the spokes I talked about before. Before it's too late. And they call that *Pte San Wi.* Later, most everybody, all us wanna-bees, everything has to be clean, pure white, call it Calf Woman, White Woman, Calf White Woman or whatever it is. *Pte San Win,* it's something like fifth grade. That's how she must look when she came. We talk about the young lady of the *Pte San,* so this is an elder that came if you really do it according to the study and She is not a young one, young lady. It's an elderly lady, grandma, that came and made that altar and how to pray this way.

The Spirit was there and if you don't understand the Spirit, go to Sweatlodge. To me its kind of touchy and dangerous because if you don't know, accidentally, that Spirit will come in and hug someone, hey, that medicine man touched me. He's gone. He's settin' behind bars. That's what's happening back home. Sometimes maybe it will hold your hand. You're getting a blessing, you know? They don't understand, he touched me. That's all people need to know. He touched me then go, good-bye. So that She brought a Spiritual *Cannunpa,* Calf Pipe. So you go that route, that pipe was part of that Buffalo. That Calf Pipe we still carry with us.

And that Peace Pipe was designed by a person from Chicago, I believe. So one side has a tomahawk and pipe, Peace Pipe. It took me a while to find this out but first I was going to somehow get a hold of a Buffalo calf. I'm going to do that, make that pipe, *Cannunpa*. Here all the time She gave us this. We are a part of that Buffalo family. I don't eat Buffalo meat. I am in bad shape, I guess. But then these are part of me. Part of the Creation. And this is the best.

He said let us pray, have faith of great bread. And if Jesus said, He is the bread of life, today we are going to have part of Him. And He says He put water and He made it into blood which he called wine, my faith in that. Break bread and then the *Wakinyan* help will come to people. I have dreamed this. He is always with us, *Wanikiyapi*. But every day I live with the Spirit, I guess, it is always with me. That is something we can live on you know. But that is good. Everything is a paradox, everything is a story to us. These two people are with us all the time. *Pte San Win* and this Man they call *Wanikiya*.

Only thing, Sunday, some people go there, for what, about an hour and a half? And they come out and they forget. They throw in a dime and they expect $1,000 or what they usually get. They never appreciate, but I'm not going to talk like that. Somebody might throw a brick at me. Stone him, stone him! I'm having a piece of Christ's body right now. Cause He said, "I am the bread of life. I am the living waters." So we are having the water, we had a little sweetening though.

Mother and Godmother are sleeping right now, of these two grand kids. Remember at that time things was going to happen. Chance, and godfather, standing there, sitting there, things happen, change, but it's not destruction it is sort of new life, new beginning. I moved from the old place. I wonder how can that little house of mine, two shower rooms take care of all these people. Just think that was all camped, now you see a full house. I named a few of my great grand kids, some silly, you know. Starting to see some great grand kids. Gracious. Then this great grandson, he was late when he came, we call him *Wicahpi,* Star, but his grandpa, will give him that name at a ceremony that is coming. We will have a special song for him that's his alone. And my granddaughter has got a boy coming. So, if this keeps up so far on this island, Turtle Island, so called America, south of Canada, seven generations.

After Crazy Horse we moved. Going the other way, we moved. But one of my boys, Luke, he went to other side, yodeling country. He's the only one been out there. Her great grandpa, he was a Swede. But he was kind of weak, he only had one wife. My great grandfather, he had five wives. Mother's side, American wife, he had four. I have proof. I have picture of them. Know all for over half century.

If you lie, you steal, steal the strength.

Time to talk about the Circle. I guess that Circle was taken away from the Lakota people, Spotted Tail, Fools Crow, he bring back. The government said no more sacrifice themselves and that was brought back 1700 or 1800 to now 1917, 1918 somewhere and they put it to work. Came to the 20's, 30's, 40's, 50's, 60's, 70's, 80's, 90's, year 2000. So, I never really found out till March pow-wow, Denver, from Red Cloud. There's good people out there, that's the main Circle. There are shaman, make believers, imitators, but I am watching, hanging on taking care of this main Circle. It's always been that way. I call this Eagle Nest, sitting out here, all this you're suppose to have. One of these mountains is 160 acres. There are Buffalo, Elk, and whatever and people whose name was Lakota. So we have that out there but who cares, I don't know where it's at but it's here.

All the single ones are my wife's, especially my sister and even though they all lose an ounce they gain about 2000 wrinkles I see, but still I was always there for him, but who cares. One of my grand kids was acreage counting 1,150 acres out there somewhere. They were skiing and all that but who cares. I am rich, these young people are rich, still, but these are not mine. The only important thing I have is this here body of mine. And the Body is the temple of the Spirit.

Do not lie. If you lie, you steal, steal the strength. It's riddle for something for faith. You go here and there. You don't dishonor. Love is what's stuck with me. Don't talk about earthquake, floods, fire. Talk about something of the future so the youngest will have a future. Throw all that in there. Elders will try to forget and middle age they take something that will make them forget. Some kind of fire, water, coffee and whatever. I'm a smoker and I might do something else to make me sort of forget. The good book says I will not send angels anymore. That crazy Indian that prays that He comes now. So tonight say some prayers. The owl takes care of us at night when it comes out. The snake is laying all around protecting us. The swift hawk, it's there. Coming in, there's also many eagles, the closer we get, a huge one, so awesome.

He said, "I will be with you even unto the end."
Maybe I get touched, maybe get healed. Maybe He
didn't pity me and give me like working people annual
vacation, couple hours this and that and maybe something I draw on. I am a human being. Like this I don't
have to come out this way, I guess. On the way out I
was thinking and I didn't do much talking. Is this my
last trip or what? Then I got to thinking, ohh, this is
kinda hard. Maybe next time I'll start flying. Then I got
to thinking like there is people like my niece, forsake
all, everything, even her Mom and Dad to go out there
and she got in and started helping drive. She forgot her
things that suppose to keep her healthy. But they fol-
lowed me. "And I promise," I said, "I'll be there. I may
be one hour early or late but by noon I should be there."
And hopefully we will make it, high noon I'll be there.

That one, he talk about the *Mahto*, the bear, somehow the bear just the word bear and the Spirit is here.
We talked about all of *pejuta,* it all here. And when you
have all that, you just have it all. This is what keeps
them going. If I step over I am already there. One foot
there and one foot here. Tomorrow I don't know what
I am going to say maybe I can bring Red Skeleton in.
Maybe a little Bob Hope. I always did like that other
one. But maybe his Spirit is up here. On the Lakota
side there is *Tunkasila* the Spirit of me. The main man
be there. Maybe somebody out of there will come back
and I'll be understood.

Life's decisions you are there, you make every moment. all you have is that moment. Each you decide what happens. That future comes in. It's the future, that road goes both ways, which way. That cigarette, that drink, or whatever, they keep you from that right. Let those go, you go deeper into the way, Sacred way. Whatever way, there's no way back to that fork. Wake up, have coffee, whatever, keep that mind on that moment.

We got to learn something. So, I have three dreams and these dreams I'm gonna share with people. The fourth one is very *Wakan.* I have no business touching it but I did. Maybe I was too loaded and stuck my head in it. The beauty one was a dream in the blue light, red and white. I finally found my true color, it is yellow and white. Somehow these two are cut off now. I have these two. One day I will be standing against the white. I know people that calls me bad mouth and white eyes. We were supposed to be very mean, Crazy Horse on father's side, Dad's side, that's where the white eyes come in. Her Dad, Two Bulls, he takes care of the *Cannunpa.* I don't care how they pray all over, it's time we prayed like this. If you don't pray, everything's like that. You pray, it will be peaceful as a child. Dad will say I hope you learn something.

This year is gonna be a lot of things coming up. I said, "Let us go after wood." Nobody did. No ash, no nothing. So how do you do this? Jokingly he says just cut that tree, *Mitaku Oyasin* and it will go over. That man pulled that tree down, push that tree down, said that's for kids. So something started at one time. So he was gonna do it, but he had a woman that had no ears, no *pejuta*. Wanna dance so bad that he went out back and said, "Oh, no, no. You want to die, go die. You're gonna die up here. You want to live, you live. We always together. You die, you die alone. Meantime, get the hell out of here." He still here.

First time I met her she was beautiful. Pretty lady standing there, ohhhh, my. She had all the colors. Everything and this and that. Look at this one, these are shiny black eyes. I was suckered in. When I got there he gave me a sack of Bull Durham. Later she said, "Don't be smoking, you gonna have cancer." I don't understand that, you know. She had something. She wants me to pray for her, whatever. Do not tell.

So I give her name out here, I don't know, several years ago. Nobody wants to be grandma, talk about wisdom. Been there longer than everybody. You know or he should know. I don't know, I guess they were having a *Cannunpa*, dancing out under the moon and stars. Government found out they call that ghost dance.

Be careful when you do that, the people said, something come into your body. I can do that if you give me $5,000 some night. I can make them dance all night. But what is that going to accomplish? Moon is for the women, the sun is for everybody.

My name is *Oyate Nawicakcijin,* Defends People, defending or protecting them, the people will depend  on him. My Lakota name. I don't know what I doing with a French name, Dubray, but at that time government say we had too. I guess it's easier to spell or maybe say. Learn all our ABC's and D's whatever. All these people that came from 100 nations, they talked about it. It's all there. To make this America. We made America what it is today. If you look at it, it isn't just a hand full of people. The English have their tradition, the British, the German, go on and on with tradition. Combine all that into just one, one egg and who create that egg? Was it Jimmy? It comes back to God again, one God. How did he come about that He is God? Where did He come from?

That Jesus was worried about us, cause He must have thought us real little bitty people, you know? So I guess in other words no matter how educated you are, what you think you know, you got to jump in there start exploring Spirit world. What Spirit I was looking for, I was looking for in each person, each other, over every-thing, the whole works.

159

This Holy Bible, it says Jesus did *Hanbleceya* the Lakota way, right here. He suppose to be happy but His body is hungry, and thirsty and sleepy and wants to be loved and rub my back, and life goes on, you know? Forget about the Spirit, everything is here, that one said to Him.

They call it island, Turtle Island, Canada, South America and here. And everything, these people are sort of open mind I guess. In other words, they always had their hearts open, welcome. They never use the word my or I. They use the word ours and we. They never claim anything, all things were given to them by God, not given to them, but to take care of them. And He says not to add anything or take anything out. Leave it the way it is, but beautify it. It's beautiful but you add beauty on it.

Now days, they started using the word my. My land, that's mine an individual mine, not ours. Go way back there about 150 years whenever, there's people coming in, take what's good and leave what's not good. Learn, take it and learn, and then return help man. That's how Chief Red Cloud talks. What he meant by that is the education is very important. They will come in groups. What he meant in groups he was talking about the religion.

He accept only one, that was the Catholic Church. The rest of them come in groups, like he said, the Episcopalian, Presbyterian and on and on. Finally, they start using the name like Church of God. Like politics, they use man made rules and, who is the first *winkte* we have here in America? The Catholic Church brought in the *Winkte*, the priests or brothers or whatever they are. None of them have a woman. So called sisters they are always together, no man, no priests talk to them but that is just a joke. Those are confidential, you know?

Then they talk about Jesus Christ, these people came and said that the Native American Indian are doing devilish work. They don't know anything about God, they created God themselves. Then they stop all our religion. When you talk about religion, religion is powerful. Now that don't make sense, does it? Religion. But they call it religion. The little groups there. Then they start talking about culture. Lots of little groups get together start smooching.

But the Native American Indian is crazy I guess. Stood there on the beach, welcome everybody, so excited, he wants to share this thing with everybody. To cut it short, one day, there were women washing their clothes, use lake, stream, whatever, kids are swimming. I talk about washing clothes; I guess they are buckskin. The only way they can clean those is by rubbing against rock, tap them a little bit on a piece of rock, of course, they had soap you know, yucca.

All of a sudden a young man came out of the water, the kids are all excited, the women are all excited, young men sitting along the hillside. They're attached to Him and He is with them many years. Always taught about the future, talked about the stars and all those stories. Even up to where we are at. He talked about the things that were going to happen. But one day He was pretty lonely, sad, and He told all the people that He was going to leave for awhile, but I'll be back. I have to go where there's other people, but they're not like you, you people. These people have started making images, they are creating gods and they are starting to move away from tabernacle.

Many years later He came back, He was all beat up, all scratched, holes in His wrists and it was told that nails were put in His hands, but that's not it, it was His wrists. Big thing going on, I guess. He was dead but He lived again, but He went on about how He appeared to His people through being a baby, He grew up with them. And His adopted Dad was a builder, carpenter. And His adopted mother, that is her with a broken heart. He said in Spirit this is where she lives. Dressed in black, in mourning, and then that pure white. I guess that's where the Catholic sisters get their colors. Never been told where He came from. He taught them many things, how to pray. He stood on top of the hill and reached down and this is how He prayed. They called it the Lords Prayer. He gave that to the people. This is how you pray to me and you shall receive.

Wherever He goes the people said, He repeats the Lords Prayer. Not His, He gave it to the people. So this is how you will see me when I come back. I'm just a short ways away. My peace I leave with you. I will always be with you, but a comforter will come and when it comes, listen and you shall receive whatever you ask and my Dad will give it to you. Now, that don't make sense. He had the power but His Dad you ask anything in His name and the Comforter came.

Later on, how can a man comfort people. Only time I get comfort is by a woman with their love, somehow when they touch like bring memories back of mother. When you're sick She's there for you. When She came She looked like beautiful girl, elderly, grandma came. That's when She taught about the altar, how to pray, what to put there. There is one thing I will not use angels anymore. I'll take them out. So you don't practice that angel, but those people they do practice that. They say I have seen an angel, it stood there, it came. But He says I will not use angels, but there our ego comes in, like She said.

My peace I leave with you.

There is this lady that came to our tribe as a comforter and brought the Holy Spirit, *Ta nagi Wakan*. She taught us about peace, talked about the White Calf Woman, She brought us Spiritual things. That's why if you close your fist, bend your elbow, you have your *Cannunpa* with you.

That *Cannunpa* means the smoking of wood. That don't make sense. You take *cansasa*, red willow and that smell. If I load a *Cannunpa* in here Grandma will probably run me out, no smoking in here. And it says take off your shoes this is *Wakan*, this is *Wakan Cannunpa*, this is Holy Man. How many people walk in the streets without shoes? You got to practice what you preach. Don't take it seriously, there are certain places that are *Wakan*.

I don't like to wear moccasins in, we're imitators, we're shaman, we try to practice some place out there. Well, no wonder, when you are stoned you crucified him. *Tunkasila, Wakan kaga.* When I go through it I say I feel *akegalkiya,* stretch out arms, hands. I see my Dad, now *Wacinmaksape, aware of Him.* I see my mother, my *Kunsi Wakan,* so I take my shoes off.

The burning bush, paperwork, I usually use my cigarette lighter be part of that. All got to be careful when we go out there. Make sure you know what is happening. People are confused about these little groups. Like they say God has many names, Mahatma, Allah,

Mohammed, they use that, black people start using that, like Mohammed and then there are the monks, they pray to somebody just like the Mormons, Mr. Smith. But we added the man made rules.

For those monks the last test is the fire going up, the hole in the fire, the ashes. You stick your hand in it and it don't burn anything, not even your face. Just like the Sweatlodge we have and the rocks we have. If a man touch those rocks, or pick up those from there, he has the faith of a God. At that moment he can touch   anything, whatever it is and it can be healed.

He said, "My Spirit will always be with you." So first time he came to me in later years, little tiny hand and leather cup. Where does this leather cup come from, where are these cups. There was a little tiny hand, there was smudge, I mean talk. One of my brothers grabbed my hand and it was broke. "Brother-in-law," he says, "grab that hand and hold it cause when the lights come on you'll be alright." All of a sudden he broke my hand. He said, "That hand was starting to get like a little tiny baby hand." So we don't know. We see ourselves like adults but to Him we're just babies. The hand has a lot to heal. Now you do this, take both hands from my wrist, pull it towards you. That pull, like this, like that, you close your eyes as you doing this, maybe a couple of times. They say, if it's blue they are stuck here, *luta* means red. One supposed to be blue and one red.

Today going to be a good day. But that little man might be with him. Thanks for helping him. The Master we call him, the woman are always there, listening, children, man, to make fun of him but He sits in the house of worship not a house of merchandise and He takes a pouch with you and look into it if there is nothing in it. "Don't worry about it," He says. "I will take care of it, coming and going." He must travel always, especially now in Spirit. Like right now there's UFO's they call them. Many things happen, earthquake, fire, flood since the beginning of time. If we didn't have television nobody could kind of stretch those stories. We went through the Trail of Tears, every day you walk through it. Like a young man walk out this morning and forgot. He is different. You see something wrong in his future but he kept on going into the future. Be open to everyone.

Just like the twelve people He choose when He gave each one a different way of worship, then He told them to respect that, then when they go to the next place hopefully no regret. We are all going to end up one big Circle with that hoop of Eagle feathers I have at Sundance ground, 101 nation they call it. Some of those people I'll never see again and they'll never see me again.

People limit where Jesus was, not realizing he can be everywhere at once.

The Aboriginal people say Jesus was there. People limit where Jesus was, not realizing he can be everywhere at once.

Grandfather said, "We're all in there. Look out probably like this, this holy thing. We're all in there." He said, "Many of us are blind, think like mud, open your eyes and ye shall see the light." What really blinds us is the thing of the world that He create. Many of them can give this to the whole and go into the future with Him. I work hard, I can't do that, that's not what He meant. He said, "You have all of this, but teach so these people are given same thing." That's why we have these generations. We try to teach and we try to tell.

Education is important and you got to work to earn it, whatever you earn is yours and then again really not yours. There are so many beautiful churches like that one in Los Angeles made out of crystal or whatever it is, you know. Some have a University; we don't need that. You have one out here, all this space here, it's all here. Next thing is, is it properly used?

The minute you know that *Tunkasila* hears, then that prayer is done.

How many people have you taught about these things we talk about? How many? Or is it just like the kingdom of his place? Certain ones go in and then shut the door. Or is it open to anybody who is seeking knowledge? You let people in and out like this before you know it respect is gone and that is relation of Mother Earth. It is really hard to understand.

I don't know, whatever I think, seems like it has come true. Mountains can move, if you believe, then all is done. Prayers are always answered. The minute you know that *Tunkasila* hears, then that prayer is done. The heart comes in here, not the mind. The colors, the Four Directions, black, red, yellow, and white. Those are Grandfathers. When we make those prayer ties, *Wopahta,* we use these. When we do this, like this those prayers are always answered. Then there's the colors from that rainbow. The heart must be there, wrap that heart round that offering. That prayer carries you. That prayer that's you, you become that. The Eagle comes in here. Many colors from that rainbow. That rainbow it's Tunkasila's promise, hope is there.

I was asked, if I've been this and did that. In time and like that, it will probably quit snowing sometime tonight. But I wanted it to stop right now, so those boys there, they'd have a lot of respect, you know. My son asked how long are they going to stay and I didn't know, so I said, probably a week. And he said, that was good.

Things have changed, but I'm probably gonna see people here the first of June. It's going to be a powerful thing this year. I don't care how you dress, you can wear bikinis or all that bouncing around, but I sit there in the past, respect, you know. I see women come without skirts, no bra, they stand there bouncing around in there. Some are grapefruit size, some baseball size, or golf ball size and all kind of sizes. It's suppose to be sacred you know. What they should do is take that shawl and cover their shoulder, not their waist, cover themselves. Look at that tipi! Look at the Sweatlodge! Women should dress like that.

Slow down. Wait in the morning, no sooner is Sundance started than they come a running, you know. That Sundance is *Wakan*. Easy to wait till eight, nine o'clock, ten o'clock then come over. Take those shoes off when you come in. And instead of chair, bring a blanket or pillow to sit on. Sit on the ground, don't stand, but sit there and pray if you're gonna pray. Those that come they stand around and they bounce around. It's just like mocking the Sundancers.

So we've got to think. There's nonbelievers out there that come. They bring their chairs and they sit there with their hats on, their sunglasses on, and no offense.

A woman she straddle her legs, legs open, sitting there? That's not suppose to be like that. A man has no business sitting like that either. Sit, with your knees together. I've tried to tell, many times over and over. No chairs, but the Sundancers lay down on the ground, that doesn't matter, some of those women just lay down, like they saying, you've seen them, I guess. Sit, don't lay down. They don't care, some of their dresses are hanging up here, saying come on.

That's all they have, you know. Respect, they should respect themselves. Women respect your bodies, don't show off. Some eyes think negative thoughts when they see these things.

The body is sacred, *Wakan*. Keep the body covered, bending your knees when pick up something. When I see women bend from waist and show everything, my face it turns red. Around men keep those knees together, you don't need that from them. Myself, I've seen better things than that, but these boys they haven't. And right there, temptation, and that makes everybody weak. Women must keep that Circle closed, take care of the fire, the water, the air. Women teach these things.

So, perhaps, when we're in that Circle, I guess, we are brothers suppose to be like brothers and sisters. Not talk to each other. So these things the peoples don't understand. Try and understand Lakota, and non-Lakota, different tribe or nationalities, whoever's there, try and listen. That's *Wakan.*

When time comes, to go for that Sundance Tree, the women protect that, pick that sage spread in that Circle. They make a big feast *Maka Ina,* for our Earth Mother, choke cherry, Buffalo, and tallow. A virgin or elder women does that, in that hole before that Tree goes up. Women's prayers take that suffering, make those Buffalo Skulls seem lighter. All those that help; cooking, outhouse, feed the people, they help keep the Dancers strong.

As soon as Sundancers, or even before they come out, people come around, standing around and they watch them as they go by, you know. That's a no-no. Keep your eyes down. And after the Sundance, leave that sage alone. That sage, all those good things, and ugly things that have happened there, are in that.

171

These people they take some, they take our problems, the peoples problems back home. Do they come back with the same problem each year? So much to tell. Tell the good things. Instruct, advise people, not give them scolding, but tell the proper way.

When go to church a long time ago, women they used to sit over one side. If I remember quite correctly women used to sit on the left side, the men were always sitting on the right. The last ten or fifteen years I go to church, it's not like that, it's like saying, boy, girl, boy, girl. The family they sit together. That's good, but this family, do they really mean it, you know? They sing the songs, they pray but do they live with it 24 hours a day or 18 or at least 12 hours a day?

Maybe I should be getting some pleasure. Only pleasure I have is smoking a cigarette. Everybody has some sort of pleasure. Everyone has touched someone or been touched or been, whatever. I'm suffering. Right now I'm worried about the Arbor going up. And who's out there doing that? The only way God can get help for me is through these hearts. I'm this and that and I guess this is what it's all about.

I will be there in the Spirit world walking with my people one day.

I'm just a little beggar. I beg for money trying to
get this new land, put up playground, set up arbor, and
all that. Maybe people talk about me. Look he's going
around for money, which I haven't yet. I'm going to
wait a couple of weeks and I might have it, something
good might happen, you know. Somebody out there
might see something or feel something. It's going to
make those people happy when they see all this set up.
Hey, I was part of that. If not, they be there mocking it,
you know. Hey, I've been a Sundancer all this time and
I believe in the *Cannunpa* way and so forth. But where
were you when I was calling, you know?

I will be there in the Spirit World walking with my
people one day. Right now they don't know me. Once a
year they know me, but after that they don't know me.
So I may not know them, when that time comes. And it
would be a shame, maybe all I know about you is your
first name. I never did find out about your last name.
Maybe I was told once, but that went in one ear and one
out. Sometimes it took me a couple of years, to learn
I guess. There's some people out there, like today, she
said "You remember him?" and I have to go along. I
don't, but I said, "Huh." And I know I'm not crazy but
it's working that way.

Couple of my grand kids are walking home after school and you know I didn't recognize them. I thought there is a young man and a young lady walking, I said who are they? Here it was, Bobby. So between Bobby and that time when he was 17, where'd I go? What happened? I may be sitting here, but maybe I am traveling someplace. What would happen if I was traveling like that and this body gives out. I could just keep on traveling, and go house to house, to all these people, like the Spirit of God. He said, "I am with you always." He is with us now, the Spirit, He's here.

I think I have been crucified many times over and over. Even the Tree split, and this life, put that Tree together. When the Tree split in this life something could be done about it, those two, they put that Tree together. I was sitting in the chair, I seen what happened. Many people didn't believe or understand. Now if, something happen this year, it will happen and it's going to be powerful, I guess.

The Lakota Spirit, He is always one God, that one we all pray to. There is only one Son and He said the only way you can make it, is you have to be like me. And this is not me talking you know. This is somebody else in me now. The voice is different, I don't know if you noticed. Someone is talking. But do people understand. God, He can stand there, and talk to you, and talk to you, and talk to you, but do you understand? Like I said, we are just instruments. Give yourself to Him so He can use you.

We don't say goodby. We say *Doksha*, later.

I will always be with you.

*Real honor is remembering,
living what was taught,
walking your talk.*

We Remember

The following are incidents remembered by some of those that loved Grandpa. Notice, there are no names after the stories. Grandpa specifically said, "Leave the names off. I don't want them to get caught in their egos!"

He never said No!

He often said, "Remember that everything you do is for the People. Live so that others might live and learn."

I remember that during a difficult Sundance, at one point, someone had a pistol pointed at Grandpa's head. Everyone was real upset! The men that were there were ready to jump up and take this man down. Grandpa said, "No! Get down on your knees and pray for this man for he is showing you where you still have anger in your heart." I'll never forget this!

At this moment, I wish I had a gift with words, to put these words to music as music can touch one so deeply as you touched us so deeply. Watching you within that Sundance Circle, wrapped in a white sheet, and seeing for the first time the Holy Spirit in physical form. You, so humble, closed-eyed, walking toward the Tree of Life, surrounded in a sheath of light, your reverent face so incredibly beautiful. How does one describe the feelings in the heart? At that moment, you were a Sacred, Holy, being. Never can I doubt the existence of *Wakan Tanka* for He was truly around you, within you. *Pila maye*

Once when it was Grandma and Grandpa's anniversary, Grandpa had promised to feed the people at the pow wow. There were about five hundred. This was to happen at suppertime. About 11:30 Grandpa came to the screened door and called, "Granddaughter." She went to the door. He said, there is nobody to feed at lunch. We are going to feed in half hour. Be over there with the food at 12:00 noon. Now the soup, with large chunks of meat in it, had just been put on the open fire pits and nothing else was started. She started to open her mouth to say it was impossible, when he yelled at her.

He said, don't even think it. You know nothing is impossible. *Tunkasila* will take care of it! Well, she walked in the kitchen and said, Grandpa just said, we are going to feed in 30 minutes.

We took that food over. There was three pots of soup, 6 watermelons, 12 loaves of bread, and one bowl of canned fruit cocktail, certainly not enough to feed 500 people. Well, we served everyone twice and filled all the coffee cans the elders brought to take food home in. When we were done there was one uncut watermelon, one loaf of bread, and about three inches of soup left in one of the pots. Grandpa just looked at us and winked, then said, "Got it?"

When I first met Grandpa there was a large tumor on my neck. The doctors had said it was probably cancer. Having been asked to work with the teachers on the reservation, I asked if they had a medicine man. They said, we don't have those anymore. One evening during a talk, some one said, the medicine man is here. He went in this small room and he began to tell who he was and where the power came from. He said, that he didn't do anything *Tunkasila* did it all. He said, to take off that jewelry and prepare. There was lots of jewelry! He then lit a lighter and ran it all over his arms and hands.

The only thoughts that came were, "O boy! What have I got myself into." Then he began to run the flame all over my arms, hands, and neck. Funny thing, it didn't burn. Next he put his hands on the tumor and began to pray in Lakota. Within ten minutes the tumor was gone and never came back. That got my attention!

Here's what I remember that Grandpa taught:
The meaning of unconditional love.
Always remember to pray for yourself and
    respect yourself.
Remember to take care of the elderly and the
    children.
Be respectful of elders and attentive to their
    needs.
Mother Earth is our first mother; always care for
    her and respect all living things.
Laughter is good medicine; don't take life too
    seriously.
If you can't say something good about someone,
    just don't say anything about them.
Miracles do happen!

On Sunday evening after the last day of the Sundance, July, 1999 a small group of us, mostly family, were gathered by the tipi on the south side of the Sundance Arbor. It was also Grandmother and Grandfather Dubray's 53rd Wedding Anniversary. One of the Sundance helpers, who is a musician, had his guitar and had been singing for us. Grandma and Grandpa had been dancing and everyone was in a happy mood. One of the women had asked Grandpa about making *wasna*. There were three of us *Wasicu*, white women present and Grandpa told us he was going to teach us about how to grind dried meat. He said, "This is a real workshop."

It was storming way off to the north and we could see lightning. Grandpa told us that the *Wakinyan* had brought a great gift, he told us to look to the North. He told us we could see that gift; it is electricity. Then he said, "Use that gift, plug in your blender and use the third speed to grind the dried meat." He told us that while our ancestors had hours and hours to grind meat by hand using a stone, in these modern times we are busy and should take advantage of modern conveniences like blenders when we can.

Grandpa was a very spiritual man, he was also practical and recognized the times that we live in.

I remember the first time that I met Grandpa, he came East for Kituah. He was giving a talk to a group of people. He said, "Come to the Sundance at Pine Ridge. You find my tipi. Then it will be ok." I thought, how in the world will I find the Sundance, and more than that, where to find his tipi? That summer his tipi was in the middle of a field in South Dakota. There were many dreams of Sundance. The last one was having a Pipe filled to offer to dance. I went to his tipi with a filled pipe to ask him to pray and give an answer. A white stranger going to Grandpa to ask to dance in an ancient dance, I had seen only in my dreams. He prayed and said I had his permission to dance. He understood more than I did about my dreams, my calling to the dance, as if he could see through my white skin to the soul that was deep inside me.

Not so long after that, when we were all snowed in for three days, he gathered us all together. He said, sing that old *Cannunpa* (Pipe) song, sing in Lokota. My conscious mind had no way of knowing what song he meant. My mind was blank. I prayed and then started to sing a song that just seemed to come from no where. When the song was finished, he told me that it was an old *Cannunpa* song. He knew all along that that song was in me.

He had this way of seeing into people and knowing things.

Once he was talking about male and female relationships. He scanned the group. He said, "That one is about all dried up." He was referring to becoming a grandmother. I had just begun to have hot flashes and hadn't told anyone because I didn't know what they were. Within a year, I was "dried up" just as he had said.

What stands out the most was what he taught about being a woman, respecting myself, and remembering to pray for yourself first. Whenever he put us out on vision quests, he always reminded us to pray for ourselves first as we could do nothing for others without praying for ourselves. He always taught about love and how important that was. He always loved the song, "May the Circle be Unbroken" and I felt in my heart, that this was his prayer; that all who loved him, would love each other in the same way, and stay connected after he was gone. His words still live in my heart today.

I remember how you taught us to learn from our mistakes! That time up at Bear Butte when out of fear I hung back about going up. Fear said, "I'd go up tomorrow." You answered, "There may not be no tomorrow." The mind said, "Then it won't matter, a whit, whether I go out or not!" You probably heard that thought.

Now I know that would have been the most important thing that could ever have been done, to have walked through fear and be with God.

There was the time that you said, "Maybe the Eagles would come and visit during Sundance," and that scared the daylights out of this one, 'cause I felt unworthy. It seemed, you were pulling energy, when you were trying to give me a gift. Again, that brain chimed in, "If Spirit wanted to gift me it didn't need to come through Grandpa!" Then the girl next to me was gifted with many dreams. I knew that I missed a great gift.

When exploring giving a flesh offering, I thought, "That it wasn't necessary as I had already given my whole life to God." Then one of the elders was asked to give flesh for one who pledged and didn't, I knew it was for me.

I remember the first dance coming back to the resting area, maybe the third day, late in the afternoon after a long hard round, and some of us weren't sure we were going to make it, you gave me a thumbs up. That was like the approval I had so often wanted from my Dad and never got. So, there was a great healing which took place with that one simple gesture.

My prayer is still to always make you proud, *Tunkasila.*

Bear Butte *Hanbleceya*, I think 1995, June. There was a bunch of us in a group, about 10-20, going to "fast" or "support" in all the various ways required. There were also some local Lakota families camped around Grandpa and Grandma's camp. This was the afternoon before the day, a bunch of us were to be put out with just tobacco on the ground marking our individual *Hocoka's*, circles, up on the Sacred Butte.

Grandpa was in a serious mood sitting in a folding chair on a relatively flat area about twenty yards below the *Inipi* lodge. Grandpa was doing a little joking, sometimes at one of our expenses, so the mood was not all that somber and we were all having some good laughs. Anyway, there were a good ten or twelve of us sitting on the earth or rocks surrounding him and periodically he was telling a story and doing most of the talking as only he could do. We were listening pretty closely as he was talking with respect about some of the Spirit beings that protect the butte and sometimes visit those fasting and praying. He was wearing a yellow, almost translucent ring on the small finger of his left hand. A few times, as he was talking, he gestured with his hand in a way that looked like he was intentionally trying to draw our curiosity to the ring. None of us were bold enough to ask him about it. He made a point of referring to it and then having us all take a close look at it. From a solid piece of amber it seemed a ring had been shaped and inside the ring was a very small ant.

Grandpa was pleased with the ring and said he wore it for all of us so we would know how to approach the Spirits if they visited any of us while we were fasting. Then he told us how he came to understand that he was actually smaller in importance than the ant. While he was praying with his

Cannunpa and fasting, a small ant came to him and grew giant size in front of him and spoke to him about important matters. I guess those matters were personal because I don't remember him elaborating on anything other than the humility aspect of seeking Spiritual guidance.

Summer 1993 we were all resting quietly after Sundance. Grandfather had spent many hours on his feet and was experiencing some pain in his hip. We had built a fire in anticipation of a *Wopila Inipi*. The fire was hot and the rocks were turning white. He was sitting in the living-room relaxing with his sons. The pain in his hip was a nuisance, but his sons were trying their best to make him comfortable. Grandfather's second youngest son was sitting beside him and wanted to tend to his father's needs. He spoke of a warm rock to soothe the hip muscle. A young, Middle Eastern boy was sitting with us and someone spoke of the rocks again. The young man volunteered to get one. Grandpa's son said, "Yeah, go get a hot rock." Since the fire was at the far end of the yard, we waited patiently. When we heard this "ouch, oh, oh, ah, ouch!" We looked up, the young man was carrying the hot rock in his bare hands.

He kept it moving and you could see smoke coming off his hands. "Ouch! Ouch!," in the door he came. Grandfather asked, "Why didn't you use horns or a pitch fork?" His response was, "You didn't tell me to so I knew I didn't need to." Love, huh!!!

Bear Butte, 1995 was especially cold. The winds blew, with rain and snow taking turns falling. The weather did not dampen the heart of the people or its leaders. It did test us! In the middle of fire duty on the second night the other fireman and myself were sitting under cover and watching the fire from a short distance. We were talking and sharing stories about our lives and making a new friendship. We told a few jokes and remarked how lucky we were to be on fire duty because we at least had heat. As the night wore on we were getting sleepy when we noticed someone standing in front of the fire. The fireman exclaimed, "Oh! It's Jim Dubray." We quickly scrambled to our feet because we never saw anyone coming up the trail. We greeted him and he asked if we were ok and we shared our good fortune by being by the fire. His response was that is why I'm here. You boy's got the best job, then he laughed. We asked how we could make him comfortable. I'm okay.

At which point we decided to sit in the lodge with a couple of warm Grandfather Rocks. He was grateful and offered some prayers for all those high up on the Butte. He prayed for all things and offered smoke. Then we settled down to enjoy the warmth of the grandfathers. We were sharing stories and Grandfather was sharing his thoughts and good feelings. The other fireman had fallen asleep. He responded, "Gee, I must be boring." We continued to talk and shared good feelings about life. I told him how sad I was about my father's passing. He showed the way to let go and to live on in respect. Later, we both had fallen asleep. Everyone was looking for him!

Sundance 1992 Grandfather Dubray spent much time teaching about our responsibilities and duties. He always emphasized that each person had a duty and place in the Circle of life. He reminded all of us many times that not everyone should dance, only those who had been called by the Great Spirit or those who had a very special reason. He spoke of the Spirit finding all of us if we would pray and believe. Well, as he instructed I prayed hard. Sure enough, prayers were answered and Spirit told me what he had already said. Wait till it is time to dance.

Since I asked for help and prayed , down I went, shaking all over. Grandfather came over and quietly and patiently watched and told everyone, "No one dies at Sundance, only life comes through, no matter what happens to the body." Some of these things were told. I do remember a gentle touch on my back and quiet, gentle words calling me and his smiling face. He reassured me and said, sit up, you are ok. He said, that we all do our part in the many Circles of Life. We must do the part that was chosen for us and let others do what they must do. I've got large ears now.

Janesville, Wisconsin was the gathering of the White Buffalo and Eagle hoop. Grandfather had many surprises, mostly pleasant. We all teased him about being chef because of a misprint in a booklet about the White Buffalo. Too bad the proofreader was real busy that day. He does not like to be called by titles but much prefers being a (common man). We did not miss any opportunities to call him Chef especially when we knew he would be cooking something up for us. The day was particularly hot and humid when we visited the farm. Many visitors, 100 as I remember, from all over the world had gathered.

The 100 were Spiritual leaders from all parts of the globe. It was decided by all the leaders that two *Inipis,* Sweatlodges, would be built that day to accommodate the visitors. Grandfather brought the news that there are no tools, no willow, no rocks, no covers but we want two lodges built by 7 p.m. It was now 3 p.m. He said, have fun and listen to yourself. Many hands pitched in, many people began to hustle around until we found everything we needed. We were all a little late but then again so was everyone else.

Chef Dubray and other dignitaries were the first to purify. Somehow the 100 rocks got very hot. With a new shallow pit the roots of the grass began to smolder and smoke. The grasshoppers were the first one's out of the lodge, they didn't ask for the door they came out from any opening. It wasn't long before the door came up. "Gee, it's smoky in here," he laughed.

I remember the woman that came to Kituah that first year with cancer, barely alive and asked for Grandpa's help. Then she came back the next year cured and healthy looking.

One of those first years at Sundance I remember seeing the thunder beings at a distance, heading toward the sacred grounds. Dark, gray clouds rolling, rumbling across the sky, then to my amazement watching the clouds split in half, passing around each side of the dance grounds and again, come together, once on the other side of the field. Now, years later, I am still in awe.

Grandfather, had many methods of teaching, but one that stands out most happened at Bear Butte. It was a particularly difficult time that year. It was very cold, wet, snowy, and muddy. Most of us were pretty miserable but trying to keep in good spirits. Two people left and went to a motel. Some were wanting to follow, but trying to remain committed to being tough and staying the night at Bear Butte. You read our thoughts, heard our needs. That was when you started saying that this way (the Lakota way) was a hard path to follow. You criticized this person, used them as an example of not being strong, of not walking the way. Later we realized you had asked this person to get a motel room for you and Grandmother.

I saw a shift happen in the people. You saying what you did gave strength to us, an inner determination. You taught us that the strong ones are sometimes used in this way for teaching examples.

I recall a time when we were blocked in by cars after attending a funeral. We were ready to leave, we waited awhile. No one came to move the cars around us, so you maneuvered your van, freeing us to drive on or, more correctly, you maneuvered the space around us to free the van. I saw limitations, you didn't. How many other limitations do we perceive are surrounding us which aren't truly there?

One afternoon Grandfather asked to go driving. As he drove we spoke of many things. At one point he asked how things were going in his house. I told him everything was fine. He asked if there was anything that had bothering me. So, I told him about that morning when a young man came up while the bacon was cooking and said the bacon had not been cooked the right way the morning before. He liked his bacon crunchy and it had been soggy. I told Grandfather that I had wanted to hit that man over the head with the spatula.

Grandfather laughed and asked, why had I not apologized and asked nicely if he would show me how he likes his bacon cooked so it could be done correctly, hand him the spatula and then walk away. This made me laugh uproariously! How clever, and how in the Spirit that would have been.

At a gathering, there were about 90 people present. Grandpa was talking to the people about building a new Sundance arbor. He wanted to build it out of wood instead of using the trees on the reservation. He was concerned that all the trees would be used up by all the other Dances that had started up. There were a lot. He had hoped that the new arbor would last 100 years and that some trees would be saved. A man that had came to hear Grandpa speak stood up and said that he would take care of the wood and not to worry about it. He even said that he would bring the wood up to South Dakota. Grandpa was very happy to hear that. Everyone thought that was nice. About 5 to 6 weeks later the wood was delivered to Grandpa and the man expected to be paid. Grandpa was so hurt and this man did not have a clue what he had done. So Grandpa paid him. It was not cheap. When the man was told that he had insulted Grandpa he quickly backed out of what he said to Grandpa.

When others got word of what had happened, they spoke to the man about what he had done. They told him that Grandpa believed he would take care of the wood, and that he was not true to his word, he was not humble. The arbor was built just like Grandpa wanted. It is still there today.

When Grandpa spoke to a group, he always preferred people in a Circle of life. Grandpa and Grandma always said to learn Indian, learn the songs, songs are prayers. Sing the lodges in order to have your prayers answered. When you go on the hill to fast, you need to know the songs to ask the Spirits for help. He always said to feed and clothe the Spirits. Take care of them, they are your relations. Grandpa always told us to be careful of what we asked for because we may get it.

He watched the weather channel almost every day, but when someone asked about the weather, he would tell them to go outside to see the weather.

Grandpa would teach or correct people by speaking past them to others, to discuss an event or moment which displeased him, which would be over heard by the misguided person without hurting or embarrassing them.

195

When Grandpa and Grandma visited, we learned a lot. The one thing that stays in our minds is the talk that he gave at the American Indian Center. There were over 150 people there that night. A lot of whites and some local Native Americans. He talked about *Tunkasila*, respect, love, and etc.....

You know how he was, anyway, there was a Native American woman who had a child that was very disabled. Grandpa, called her up to the front with her child and asked the people who were sitting at front table with him to put their hands on the boy and pray with him. Everyone prayed and there was not a dry eye in the house. There was so much love expressed for that child by all the people there. The energy was so powerful.

Early that evening, after feeding the elders. Grandpa walked passed this huge plate of food that had been offered to the Spirits. He looked down at the plate and said, "OHHHHH! You are feeding the homeless too." The women that had put out the Spirit food were so embarrassed.

The next day, the boys, Grandpa always called the men that, who had gathered at the Sweatlodge, were told by grandfather to place eleven rocks in the fire. He returned to the house. They placed sixty rocks in the fire thinking that he would need more due to the large number of people. After the water-pourer asked for all of the *Inyans* to be brought in, people began crawling under the tarps in all directions. Grandpa said, "I asked for eleven rocks, you don't listen." He always suggested that to listen and you might learn something. We remember one year at Bear Butte when a young lady had given Grandpa her lawn chair to sit on. She decided to leave before the ceremony was concluded and asked for her chair back. When Grandpa got up and she took possession of her chair, her skirt caught fire and flames rose up her back until she was rolled on the ground to extinguish it.

I remember this woman came out of the lodge with a vision of a grandmother fussing at her. Someone took her to Grandfather and she shared the vision with him. He looked at the confused woman, laughed and said, "It's going to be very hard, but learn." He patted her hand and walked off laughing at what this woman had gotten herself into.

Grandpa was always using tricks and talking in circles to get our attention. He would tell us to get ready for a Sweatlodge, then ask why we were sitting around indecent. Many times he would tell us to do one thing then yell at us for not doing the opposite. I remember the year he ask us to bring him a lemon meringue pie on the plane from North Carolina, then ask us to take it out on the hill at Bear Butte. It took years to understand that one. Sometimes he would criticize someone, or use them as an example, when they were the one doing it right. At the time if you were the one being criticized it was hard to remember he needed your help. Once out at Sundance he walked up and began yelling at me about anything and everything. When he was all done, he smiled and said, "I just needed to yell." When we made mistakes, he would say, "Forget it. You can stay back there or you can walk up here beside me." Although he taught in a hard way, everything he did was for our growth. There was not a time when we did not know that he loved all of us more than we could ever imagine.

James Dubray, or Jimmy Dubray as friends called him, was Grandfather to many of us. When he came to visit, He stood on the deck, looked out over the woods and mountains and said, "This is good, I want to bring my whole family here." I said bring them on, not knowing what the future impact this man and his family would have on life. He said "You don't know what you asking for, I have a Big family." That was in the winter of 1991.

The next Fall, his family came. There were over forty Lakota's of all ages, it was good. Over the next ten years many hours were spent visiting with that old man. Hours watching the sunrise propped in chairs in front of his home on the reservation drinking coffee, hours on long and short drives, hours at the kitchen table, and hours in ceremony. He talked about the ways of his people. He'd would gently scold, for not respecting what was sacred. He taught how to love life and all my relations, both through words and example. Most of all he taught me how to laugh at myself. He was a teacher, relative, and friend. I still see that tinkle in his eye and grin on his face.

One of the fondest memories is when he would offer a handshake, but instead point a finger back at me. "Gotch ya," he would say.

He never had an unkind word to speak of any person or thing. He loved life and taught everyone around him what *"Mitaku Oyasin"* meant.

Never Be Afraid!

Grandfather James Dubray